# Oracle PL/SQL Best Practices

# Oracle PL/SQL Best Practices

Steven Feuerstein

Beijing · Cambridge · Farnham · Köln · Paris · Sebastopol · Taipei · Tokyo

### Oracle PL/SQL Best Practices

by Steven Feuerstein

Published by O'Reilly & Associates, Inc., 101 Morris Street, Sebastopol, CA 95472.

**Editor:** Deborah Russell

**Production Editor:** Mary Anne Weeks Mayo

**Cover Designer:** Ellie Volckhausen

**Printing History:**

    April 2001:       First Edition.

ISBN: 0-596-00121-5

[M]

*To the many Israeli and Palestinian women
who reject the violence of Israel's military
occupation and have dedicated their lives to
work for a just and lasting peace*

—Steven Feuerstein

# Table of Contents

# *Preface*

When I first started writing about the Oracle PL/SQL language back in 1994, the only sources of information were the product documentation (such as it was) and the occasional paper and presentation at Oracle User Group events. Today, there are at least a dozen books that focus exclusively on PL/SQL, numerous products that help you write PL/SQL code (integrated development environments, knowledge bases, etc.), training classes, and web sites. And the community of PL/SQL developers continues to grow in size and maturity, even with the advent of Java.

Access to information about PL/SQL is no longer the challenge. It can, on the other hand, be difficult to make sense of all the new features, the numerous resources, the choices for tools, and so on. When it comes to writing a program or an entire application, developers have, over and over again, expressed the desire for advice. They ask:

- How should I format my code?

- What naming conventions, if any, should I use?

- How can I write my packages so that they can be more easily maintained?

- What is the best way to query information from the database?

- How can I get all the developers on my team to handle errors the same way?

So many questions, so much burning desire to write code well, and so few resources available to help us do that.

So I decided to write a book that offers a concentrated set of "best practices" for the Oracle PL/SQL language. The objective of this book is to provide concrete, immediately applicable, quickly located advice that will assist you in writing code that is readable, maintainable, and efficient.

You will undoubtedly find recommendations in this book that also appear in some of my other books; I hope you will not be offended by this repetition. It's simply impossible to offer in a single book everything that can and should be written about the Oracle PL/SQL language. While I plan to reinforce these best practices in the appropriate places in my other texts, I believe that we will all benefit from also having them available in one concise book, a book designed, beginning to end, to give you quick access to my recommendations for excellent PL/SQL coding techniques.

## *Structure of This Book*

*Oracle PL/SQL Best Practices* is composed of nine chapters and one appendix. Each chapter contains a set of best practices for a particular area of functionality in the PL/SQL language. For each best practice, I've provided as many of the following elements as are applicable:

*Title*
> A single sentence that describes the best practice and provides an identifier for it in the form *XXX-nn* (where *XXX* is the type of best practice—for example, EXC for exception handling—and *nn* is the sequential number within this set of best practices); see the section "About the Code" for how to use this identifier online. I have, whenever possible, sought to make this title stand on its own. In other words, you should be able to glance at it and understand its impact on how you write code. This way, after you've read the entire best practice, you can use Appendix A, *Best Practices Quick Reference* (or the pull-out quick-reference card), to instantly remind you of best practices as you write your code.

*Description*
> A lengthier explanation of the best practice. It's simply not possible to cover all the nuances in a single sentence!

*Example*
> We learn best from examples, so just about every best practice illustrates, through code and/or anecdote, the value of the best practice. Whenever it makes sense, I put the example code in a file that you can use (or learn from) in your own programming environment. You'll find these files on the O'Reilly web site (see "About the Code" later in this Preface).

*Benefits*

Why should you bother with this best practice? How crucial is it for you to follow this particular recommendation? This section offers a quick review of the main benefits you will see by following the best practice.

*Challenges*

Wouldn't it be great if we lived in a world in which following a best practice was all-around easier than the "quick and dirty" approach? That is, unfortunately, not always the case. This element warns you about the challenges, or drawbacks, you might face as you implement the best practice.

*Resources*

In the world of the Internet, everything is connected; no programmer stands alone! This section recommends resources, ranging from books to URLs to files containing code, that you can use to help you successfully follow this best practice. Where filenames are shown in this section, they refer to files available on, or referenced by, the O'Reilly web site.

Here are brief descriptions of the chapters and appendix:

Chapter 1, *The Development Process*, steps back from specific programming recommendations. It offers advice about how to improve the overall process by which you write code.

Chapter 2, *Coding Style and Conventions*, offers a series of suggestions on how to format and organize your code so that it is more readable and, therefore, more maintainable.

Chapter 3, *Variables and Data Structures*, takes a close look at how you ought to declare and manage data within your PL/SQL programs.

Chapter 4, *Control Structures*, is a "back to basics" chapter that talks about the best way to write IF statements, loops, and even the GOTO statement! Sure, these aren't terribly complicated constructs, but there are still right and wrong ways to work with them.

Chapter 5, *Exception Handling*, covers another critical aspect of robust application development: exception handling, or what to do when things go wrong.

Chapter 6, *Writing SQL in PL/SQL*, focuses on the most crucial aspect of PL/SQL development: how you should write the SQL statements in your programs.

Chapter 7, *Program Construction,* offers advice on how best to build your procedures, functions, and triggers—the program units that contain your business logic. It also includes best practices for parameter construction.

Chapter 8, *Package Construction,* steps back from individual program units to present recommendations for packages, the building blocks of any well-designed PL/SQL-based application.

Chapter 9, *Built-in Packages,* focuses on how to take best advantage of a few of the most often used of the packages provided to us by Oracle Corporation.

Appendix A, *Best Practices Quick Reference,* compiles the best practice titles across all the chapters into a concise resource. Once you have studied the individual best practices, you can use this appendix as a checklist, to be reviewed before you begin coding a new program or application. You'll also find a removable version of this appendix on the quick-reference card bound into the back of the book.

# *How to Use This Book*

My primary goal in writing this book was to create a resource that would make a concrete, noticeable difference in the quality of the PL/SQL code you write. To accomplish this, the book needs to be useful and usable not just for general study, but also for day-to-day, program-to-program tasks. It also needs to be concise and to the point. A 1,000-page text on best practices would be overwhelming, intimidating, and hard to use.

The result is this relatively brief (I consider any publication under 200 pages a major personal accomplishment!), highly structured book. I recommend that you approach *Oracle PL/SQL Best Practices* as follows:

1. Read the next section, "Not All Best Practices Are Created Equal." Some of the best practices in this book—whole chapters, in fact—will have a much higher impact than others on the quality and efficiency of your code. If you find that your current practices (or those of your organization) are far from the mark, then you will have identified your priorities for initial study.

2. Skip to Appendix A and peruse the best practice titles from each chapter. If you have been programming for any length of time, you will probably find yourself thinking: "Yes, I do that," and "Uh-huh, we've got that one covered." Great! I would still encourage you to read what I've got to say on those topics, as you might be able to deepen your knowledge or learn new techniques. In any case, a quick review of the appendix will allow you to identify areas that are

new to you, or perhaps strike a chord, as in "Oh my gosh, that program I wrote last week does exactly what Steven says to avoid. Better check that out!"

3. Dive into individual chapters or best practices within chapters. Read a best practice, wrestle with it, if necessary, to make sure that you really, truly agree with it. *And then apply that best practice.* This isn't an academic exercise. You will only truly absorb the lesson if you apply it to your code—if you have a problem or program that can be improved by the best practice.

If you are new to programming or new to PL/SQL, you will certainly also benefit greatly from a cover-to-cover reading of the text. In this case, don't try to fully absorb and test out every best practice. Instead, read and think about the best practices without the pressure of applying each one. When you are done, try to picture the best practices as a whole, reinforcing the following themes:

* I want to write code that I—and others—can easily understand and change as needed.

* The world is terribly complex, so I should strive to keep my code simple. I can then meet that complexity through carefully designed interaction between elements of my code.

Then you will be ready to go back to individual chapters and deepen your understanding of individual best practices.

The other crucial way to take advantage of this book is to *use the code* provided on the companion web site. See the later section "About the Code," for detailed information on the software that will help you bring your best practices to life.

## *Not All Best Practices Are Created Equal*

This book contains about 120 distinct recommendations. I could have included many, many more. In fact, I filled up a Rejects document as I wrote the book. Following the proven, "top-down" approach, I first came up with a list of best practices in each area of the language. Then I went through each area, filling in the descriptions, examples, and so on. As I did this, I encountered numerous "best practices" that surely were the right way to do things. The reality, however, is that few people would ever bother to remember and follow them, and if they did bother, it would not make a significant difference in their code.

I had realized, you see, that not all best practices are created equal. Some are much, much more important than others. And some are just better left out of the book, so that readers aren't distracted by "clutter." I hope that the result—this book—has an immediate and lasting impact. But even among the best practices I didn't reject, some stand out as being especially important—so I've decided to award these best practices the following prizes:

*Grand Prize*

    **SQL-00**: Establish and follow clear rules for how to write SQL in your application. (See Chapter 6.)

*First Prize*

    **MOD-01**: Encapsulate and name business rules and formulas behind function headers. (See Chapter 7.)

*Second Prize: Two Winners*

    **EXC-00**: Set guidelines for application-wide error handling before you start coding. (See Chapter 5.)

    **PKG-02**: Provide well-defined interfaces to business data and functional manipulation using packages. (See Chapter 8.)

*Third Prize: Four Winners*

    **MOD-03**: Limit execution section sizes to a single page using modularization. (See Chapter 7.)

    **DAT-15**: Expose package globals using "get and set" modules. (See Chapter 3.)

    **DEV-03**: Walk through each other's code. (See Chapter 1.)

    **STYL-09**: Comment tersely with value-added information. (See Chapter 2.)

If you follow each of these "best of the best" practices, you will end up with applications that are the joy and envy of developers everywhere!

# *About the Code*

The best way to learn how to write good code is by analyzing and following examples. Almost every best practice offered in this book includes a code example, both in the text and in downloadable form from the Oracle PL/SQL Best Practices site, available through the O'Reilly & Associates site at:

    *http://www.oreilly.com/catalog/orbestprac*

To locate the code for your best practice, simply enter the best practice identifier, such as **BIP-10**, in the search field. You will then be directed to the associated code. You can also browse the site by topic area. You can even offer your own insights about PL/SQL best practices, so I encourage you to visit and contribute.

As a rule, I will follow my own best practices in these examples (unless the point of the code is to demonstrate a "bad practice"!). So, for example, you will rarely see me using DBMS_OUTPUT.PUT_LINE, even though this "show me" capability is needed in many programs. As I mention in **BIP-01**, you should avoid calling this procedure directly; instead, build or use an encapsulation *over* DBMS_OUTPUT.PUT_LINE. So rather than seeing code like this:

```
DBMS_OUTPUT.PUT_LINE (l_date_published);
```

you will instead encounter a call to the "pl" or "put line" procedure:

```
pl (l_date_published);
```

I also make many references to PL/Vision packages. PL/Vision is a code library, consisting of more than 60 packages that offer 1,000-plus procedures and functions to perform a myriad of useful tasks in PL/SQL applications. I have deposited much of what I have learned in the last five years about PL/SQL into PL/Vision, so I naturally return to it for examples. Any package mentioned in this book whose name starts with "PLV" is a PL/Vision package.

A completely free, "lite" version of PL/Vision is available from the PL/SQL Pipeline Archives at:

*http://www.revealnet.com/Pipelines/PLSQL/archives.htm*

Select the "RevealNet Active PL/SQL Knowledge Base" from the list. (You might also like to download and try out the other code you'll find there.) A commercial version of PL/Vision (with more packages and functionality than the lite version) is currently available inside the RevealNet Active PL/SQL Knowledge Base (*http://www.revealnet.com*).

Whenever possible, the code I provide for the book can be used to generate best-practice-based code and as prebuilt, generalized components in your applications, code that you can use without having to make any modifications.

The code examples offer programs that you can use to both generate and directly implement those best practices. In some cases, the programs are rather simple "prototypes"; they work as advertised, but you will probably want to make some changes before you put them into production applications.

And you should most certainly test every single program you use from *Oracle PL/SQL Best Practices*! I have run *some* tests, and my wonderful technical reviewers have also exercised the code. In the end, however, if the code goes into your application, you are responsible for making sure that it meets your needs.

# *Other Resources*

This book is intended to complement numerous other resources for PL/SQL developers. It is, to my knowledge, the first collection of best practices specifically for the Oracle PL/SQL language. On the other hand, it doesn't stand on its own as a comprehensive resource, either for PL/SQL, in particular, or for Oracle application development, in general.

What follows is by no means an exhaustive list of resources for developers. However, I find that a 15-page bibliography is more intimidating than it is helpful. So I offer this short list of the resources that I have recently found most useful and interesting:

*Code Complete* by Steven McConnell (Microsoft Press)
> A classic text, this "practical handbook of software criticism" should be on the bookshelf of every developer or at least in your team's library. Chock-full of practical advice for constructing code, it shows examples in many languages, including Ada, which is enough like PL/SQL to make learning from McConnell a breeze. Don't start coding without it! The web site for Steven McConnell's consulting practice, *www.construx.com*, is also packed with lots of good advice.

*Refactoring* by Martin Fowler (Addison Wesley)
> According to this book, "refactoring is the process of changing a software system in such a way that it doesn't alter the external of the code, yet improves its internal structure." Sound great, or *what*? This excellent book uses Java as its example language, but the writing is clear and the Java straightforward. There is much to apply here to PL/SQL programming.

*Extreme Programming Explained*, by Kent Beck (Addison Wesley)
> This book is a highly readable and concise introduction to Extreme Programming (XP), a lightweight software development methodology. Visit *http://www.xprogramming.com* or *http://www. extremeprogram-*

*ming.org* for a glimpse into the world of this interesting approach to development.

And then, of course, there is my own oeuvre, the Oracle PL/SQL Series from O'Reilly & Associates, which includes:

*Oracle PL/SQL Programming*, with Bill Pribyl
> The complete language reference for Oracle PL/SQL.

*Oracle PL/SQL Programming: Guide to Oracle8i Features*
> A companion volume describing the Oracle8*i* additions to the PL/SQL language.

*Oracle PL/SQL Developer's Workbook*, with Andrew Odewahn
> A workbook containing problems (and accompanying solutions) that will test your knowledge of Oracle PL/SQL language features.

*Oracle Built-in Packages*, with Charles Dye and John Beresniewicz
> A complete reference to the many built-in packages provided by Oracle Corporation.

*Advanced Oracle PL/SQL Programming with Packages*
> A description of how to write your own PL/SQL packages, including a large number of packages you can use in your own programs.

*Oracle PL/SQL Language Pocket Reference*, with Bill Pribyl and Chip Dawes
> A quick reference to the PL/SQL language syntax.

*Oracle PL/SQL Built-ins Pocket Reference*, with John Beresniewicz and Chip Dawes
> A quick reference to the calls to the Oracle built-in functions and packages.

# Conventions Used in This Book

The following typographical conventions are used in this book:

Italic
> Indicates filenames, directory names, and URLs. It's also used for emphasis and for the first use of a technical term.

Bold
> Used when referring, by number, to a best practice described in this book (e.g., **BIP-04**).

Constant width
> Indicates examples and to show the contents of files and the output of commands.

**Constant width bold**

> Indicates code entered by a user (e.g., via SQL*Plus) or to highlight code lines being discussed.

*UPPERCASE*

> In code examples, indicates PL/SQL keywords.

*lowercase*

> In code examples, indicates user-defined items (e.g., variables).

The owl icon designates a note, which is an important aside to the nearby text. For example, I'll use this icon when suggesting the use of an alternative feature.

The turkey icon designates a warning relating to the nearby text. For example, I'll use this icon when a particular feature might affect performance or preclude use of some other feature.

## *Comments and Questions*

Please address comments and questions concerning this book to the publisher:

> O'Reilly & Associates, Inc.
> 101 Morris Street
> Sebastopol, CA 95472
> (800) 998-9938 (in the United States or Canada)
> (707) 829-0515 (international/local)
> (707) 829-0104 (fax)

There is a web page for this book, which lists errata, examples, or any additional information. You can access this page at:

> *http://www.oreilly.com/catalog/orbestprac*

To comment or ask technical questions about this book, send email to:

> *bookquestions@oreilly.com*

For more information about books, conferences, software, Resource Centers, and the O'Reilly Network, see the O'Reilly web site at:

> *http://www.oreilly.com*

# *Acknowledgments*

Thanks go, first of all, to my editor of six years at O'Reilly & Associates, Deborah Russell. She got me off the dime on this project and helped me turn it around in record time (I started doing serious writing on this book in October 2000 and finished it up in January 2001). It was, once again, a real pleasure working with you, Debby!

Thanks as well to the other O'Reilly people who turned this book into a finished product: Mary Anne Weeks Mayo, the production editor; Ellie Volckhausen, who designed the cover; and Caroline Senay, the editorial assistant who helped in many ways throughout the project.

Many outstanding Oracle developers and DBAs contributed their time and expertise, through technical review, code samples, or writing. My deep-felt gratitude goes out to: John Beresniewicz, Rohan Bishop, Dick Bolz, Dan Clamage, Bill Caulkins, Dan Condon-Jones, Fawwad-uz-Zafar Siddiqi, Gerard Hartgers, Edwin van Hattem, Dwayne King, Darryl Hurley, Giovanni Jaramillo, Vadim Loevski, Pavel Luzanov, Matthew MacFarland, Jeffrey Meens, James "Padders" Padfield, Rakesh Patel, Bill Pribyl, Andre Vergison (the brains behind PL/Formatter), and Solomon Yakobson. This book benefited, in particular, from a reworking of best practice titles by John Beresniewicz, close readings of many chapters by Dan Clamage (whose excellent comments on certain best practices I've included as sidebars in the text), and the contribution of trigger best practices by Darryl Hurley.

*Oracle PL/SQL Best Practices* is a much improved text as a result of all of your assistance, my friends. Any errors, on the hand, are entirely my fault and responsibility.

I would also like to thank my wife, Veva, for volunteering to pick up Eli from Jordan's house so that I could stay behind and write these acknowledgments (oh, and also for adding layer upon layer of meaning and happiness to my life).

# 1

# *The Development Process*

To do your job well, you need to be aware of, and to follow, both "little" best practices—very focused tips on a particular coding technique—and "big" best practices. This chapter offers some suggestions on the big picture: how to write your code as part of a high-quality development process.

My objective isn't to "sell" you on any particular development methodology (though I must admit that I am most attracted to so-called "lightweight" methodologies such as Extreme Programming and SCRUM).* Instead, I'll remind you of basic processes you should follow within any big-picture methodology.

In other words, if you (or your methodology) don't follow some form of the best practices in this chapter, you are less likely to produce high-quality, successful software. I don't (with perhaps a single exception) suggest a specific path or tool. You just need to make sure you've got these bases covered.

## *DEV-01: Set standards and guidelines before writing any code.*

These standards and guidelines would, if I had my way, include many or all of the best practices described in this book. Of course, you need to make your own deci-

---

* This chapter contains numerous references to Extreme Programming resources. For more information about SCRUM, "a process for empirically managing product development and improving team productivity," visit *http://www.controlchaos.com*. Note that SCRUM isn't an acronym, but a reference to the "scrum" in the sport of rugby, a metaphor for the daily meetings that are the core of the SCRUM methodology.

sions about what is most important and practical in your own particular environment.

Key areas of development for which you should proactively set standards are:

- *Selection of development tools*: You should no longer be relying on SQL*Plus to compile, execute, and test code; on a basic editor like Notepad to write the code; or on EXPLAIN PLAN to analyze application performance. Software companies offer a multitude of tools (with a wide range of functionality and price) that will help dramatically improve your development environment. Decide on the tools to be used by all members of the development group.

- *How SQL is written in PL/SQL code:* The SQL in your application can be the Achilles' heel of your code base. If you aren't careful about how you place SQL statements in your PL/SQL code, you'll end up with applications that are difficult to optimize, debug, and manage over time.

- *An exception handling architecture*: Users have a hard time understanding how to use an application correctly, and developers have an even harder time debugging and fixing an application if errors are handled inconsistently (or not at all). The best way to implement application-wide, consistent error handling is to use a standardized package according to specific guidelines.

- *Processes for code review and testing:* There are some basic tenets of programming that must not be ignored. You should never put code into production without having it reviewed by one or more other developers, and without performing exhaustive testing. Astonishingly, many (if not most) PL/SQL development shops have neither standard, mandatory code reviews nor a strict testing regimen.

Best practices throughout this chapter and the rest of the book address these crucial aspects of software development. You will also find many relevant examples throughout the book.

### Benefits

By setting clear standards and guidelines for at least the areas just listed (tools, SQL, error handling, and code review and testing), you ensure a foundation that will allow you to be productive and to produce code of reasonable quality.

### Challenges

The deadline pressures of most applications mitigate against taking the time up front to establish standards, even though we all know that such standards are likely to save time down the line.

---

## DEV-02: Ask for help after 30 minutes on a problem.

Following this simple piece of advice will probably have more impact on your code than anything else in this book!

How many times have you stared at the screen for hours, trying this and that in a vain attempt to fix a problem in your code? Finally, exhausted and desperate, you call over your cubicle wall: "Hey, Melinda, could you come over here and look at this?" When Melinda reaches your cube she sees in an instant what you, after hours, still could not see. Gosh, it's like magic!

Except it's not magic and it's not mysterious at all. Remember: humans write software, so an understanding of human psychology is crucial to setting up processes that encourage quality software. We humans (especially the males of the species) like to get things right, like to solve our own problems, and do not like to admit that we *don't* know what is going on. Consequently, we tend to want to hide our ignorance and difficulties. This tendency leads to many wasted hours, high levels of frustration, and, usually, nasty, spaghetti code.

Team leaders and development managers need to cultivate an environment in which we are encouraged to admit what we do not know, and ask for help earlier rather than later. Ignorance isn't a problem unless it is hidden from view. And by asking for help, you validate the knowledge and experience of others, building the overall self-esteem and confidence of the team.

There is a good chance that if you spend 30 minutes fruitlessly analyzing your code, two more hours will not get you any further along to a solution. Instead, get in the habit of sharing your difficulty with a coworker (preferably an assigned "buddy," so the line of communication between the two of you is officially acknowledged and doesn't represent in any way acknowledgement of a failure).

### Example

Programmers are a proud and noble people. We don't like to ask for help; we like to bury our noses in our screen and create. So the biggest challenge to getting people to ask for help is to change behaviors. Here are some suggestions:

- The team leader must set the example. When I have the privilege to manage a team of developers, I go out of my way to ask each and every person on that team for help on one issue or another. If you are a coach to other teams of developers, identify the programmer who is respected by all others for her expertise. Then convince *her* to seek out the advice of others. Once the leader (formal or informal) shows that it is OK to admit ignorance, everyone else will gladly join in.

- Post reminders in work areas, perhaps even individual cubicles, such as "STUCK? ASK FOR HELP" and "IT'S OK NOT TO KNOW EVERYTHING." We need to be reminded about things that don't come naturally to us.

### Benefits

Problems in code are identified and solved more rapidly. Fewer hours are wasted in a futile hunt for bugs.

Knowledge about the application and about the underlying software technology is shared more evenly across the development team.

### Challenges

The main challenge to successful implementation of this best practice is psychological: don't be afraid to admit you don't know something or are having trouble figuring something out.

### Resources

*Peopleware: Productive Projects and Teams*, by Tom DeMarco and Timothy Lister (Dorset House). This is a fantastic book that combines deep experience in project management with humor and common sense.

## DEV-03: Walk through each other's code.

Software is written to be executed by a machine. These machines are very, very fast, but they aren't terribly smart. They simply do what they are told, following the instructions of the software we write, as well as the many other layers of software that control the CPU, storage, memory, etc.

It is extremely important, therefore, that we make sure the code we write does the right thing. Our computers can't tell us if we missed the mark ("garbage in, garbage out" or, unfortunately, "garbage in, gospel out"). The usual way we validate code is by running that code and checking the outcomes (well, actually, in most cases we have our *users* run the code and let us know about failures). Such tests are, of course, crucial and must be made. But they aren't enough.

It is certainly possible that our tests aren't comprehensive and leave errors undetected. It is also conceivable that the *way* in which our code was written produces the correct results in very undesirable ways. For instance, the code might work "by accident" (two errors cancel themselves out).

A crucial complement to formal testing of code is a formalized process of code review or walk-through. Code review involves having other developers actually read and review your source code. This review process can take many different forms, including:

- *The buddy system*: Each programmer is assigned another programmer to be ready at any time to look at his buddy's code and to offer feedback.

- *Formal code walkthroughs*: On a regular basis (and certainly as a "gate" before any program moves to production status), a developer presents or "walks through" her code before a group of programmers.

- *Pair programming*: No one codes alone! Whenever you write software, you do it in pairs, where one person handles the tactical work (thinks about the specific code to be written and does the typing), while the second person takes the strategic role (keeps an eye on the overall architecture, looks out for possible bugs, and generally critiques—always constructively). Pair programming is an integral part of Extreme Programming.

### Benefits

Overall quality of code increases dramatically. The architecture of the application tends to be sounder, and the number of bugs in production code goes way down. A further advantage is that of staff education—not just awareness of the project, but also an increase in technological proficiency due to the synergistic effect of working together.

### Challenges

The development manager or team leader must take the initiative to set up the code review process and must give developers the time (and training) to do it right. Also, code review seems to be the first casualty of deadline crunch. Further, a new PL/SQL project might not have the language expertise available on the team to do complete, meaningful walkthroughs.

### Resources

*Handbook of Walkthroughs, Inspections, and Technical Reviews*, by Daniel Freedman and Gerald M. Weinberg (Dorset House). Now in its third edition, this book uses a question-and-answer format to show you exactly how to implement reviews for all sorts of product and software development.

*Extreme Programming Explained*, by Kent Beck (Addison Wesley). The first book on Extreme Programming offers many insights into pair programming.

*Extreme Programming Installed*, by Ron Jeffries, Ann Anderson, and Chet Hendrickson (Addison Wesley). Focuses on how to implement Extreme Programming in your environment.

## DEV-04: Validate standards against source code in the database.

This book is chock-full of recommendations, standards, guidelines, and so on. The usual immediate, visceral response to all of these *shoulds* is: how can I possibly remember them? And how can I make sure that any of our developers actually follow through on their "shoulds?"

PL/SQL offers one big advantage in this area: all source code is stored in the database and is made available through data dictionary views (ALL_SOURCE, USER_SOURCE, DBA_SOURCE). Oracle also maintains additional information about code, such as dependencies, in other views. You can—and should—fairly easily validate at least some of the standards that you set by running queries against these views.

Here are some things you can do with this information:

- Set up a weekly job (via DBMS_JOB) to identify any programs that have changed, have been created, or have been removed in the past week. Publish this information as HTML on an intranet so developers can, at any time, be aware of these changes. This approach can improve reuse within your organization, for example.

- Provide queries, preferably organized within programs in a package, that developers can run (or, again, can be run as scheduled, weekly jobs) to check to see how well their code complies with standards.

 Executing, as well as writing, queries against data dictionary views (particularly the dependency-related views) can be time-consuming. Be patient!

## *Example*

Suppose we have agreed that individual developers should never call RAISE_ APPLICATION_ERROR directly. Instead they should call the raise procedure of the standard error-handling package (see **EXC-04**).

Here is a simple query that identifies all those program units (and lines of code) that contain this "off limits" built-in:

```
SELECT name, line || ' - ' || text code
  FROM ALL_SOURCE
WHERE UPPER (text) LIKE '%RAISE_APPLICATION_ERROR%'
ORDER BY name, line;
```

This answers a common question: "does my code have X in it?" Rather than executing these standalone queries over and over again, you will find it worthwhile to encapsulate such a query inside a packaged interface, such as this "standards validation" package:

```
CREATE OR REPLACE PACKAGE valstd
IS
    PROCEDURE progwith (str IN VARCHAR2);
    PROCEDURE pw_rae;
END valstd;
/
```

You can now call valstd.pw_rae to show all the "programs with" RAISE_ APPLICATION_ERROR (as you can easily see from the valstd package body). You can also call valstd.progwith to search for other strings. If, therefore, You've a standard that developers should never hard-code −20,000 error numbers, issue this command:

```
SQL> exec valstd.progwith ('-20')
```

and view what is likely to be a superset of all such instances.

Another kind of standard that might be set within an organization is that application code should never reference a table or view directly but instead always go through an encapsulation package (**SQL-01**). Here is a query that identifies all program units that violate this rule:

```
SELECT owner || '.' || name refs_table,
       referenced_owner || '.' ||
       referenced_name table_referenced
  FROM all_dependencies
WHERE owner LIKE UPPER ('&1')
  AND TYPE IN ('PACKAGE',
               'PACKAGE BODY',
               'PROCEDURE',
               'FUNCTION')
  AND referenced_type IN ('TABLE', 'VIEW')
ORDER BY owner,
         name,
         referenced_owner,
         referenced_name;
```

### Benefits

You don't have to rely solely on "manual" walkthroughs of code to validate compliance with group standards.

Code analysis and code "mining" (extracting information from/about source code) can be automated and tightly integrated into the development process.

### Challenges

You need to design and build the analysis code and then integrate these checks into your ongoing development effort.

### Resources

*reftabs.sql*: Query identifying direct references to tables and views.

*valstd.pkg*: Simple prototype package offering an interface to identify the presence of unwanted text in source code.

## DEV-05: Generate code whenever possible and appropriate.

Life is short—and way too much of it is consumed by time spent in front of a computer screen, moving digits with varying accuracy over the keyboard. Seems to me that we should be aggressive about finding ways to build our applications with an absolute minimum of time and effort while still producing quality goods. A key component of such a strategy is code generation: rather than write the code yourself, you let some other piece of software write the code for you.

Code generation is particularly useful when you have defined standards you want everyone to follow. You can try to get developers to conform to those standards with a "stick" approach: follow the standards, or else! But a more effective way to get the often anarchistic, or at least highly individualistic, programmer to follow standards is to make it easier to follow than not follow those guidelines. See the "Examples" section for specific demonstrations of this "carrot" approach.

In addition to helping to implement standards, code generation comes in handy when you have to write code that is repetitive in structure (i.e., it can be expressed generally by a pattern). For example, the kind of code you write to determine if there is at least one row in a table for a given primary key is the same regardless of the table (and primary key). Wouldn't it be nice to be able to call a procedure that queries the table structure and key from the data dictionary and generates the function?

How do you generate code? You can pick from one of these three options:

- Write your own custom query or program to meet specific needs. The "Examples" section steps you through a simple demonstration of how to go about this.
- Use a commercial tool that focuses on code generation. The "Resources" section offers a list of known code-generation tools for PL/SQL developers.
- Run relatively constrained, functionally specific generation utilities that others have written (noncommercial, freeware). The "Resources" section offers a list of generation utilities available on the Oracle PL/SQL Best Practices web site.

## Examples

Let's explore these three options for generation.

First, we have the classic "SQL generating SQL." Suppose that I want to drop all the tables in my schema. There is no "drop all" command. Instead, I throw together a query against USER_TABLES whose output is, in fact, a series of DROP statements, and then execute that output as a spooled file in SQL*Plus:

```
SET PAGESIZE 0
SET FEEDBACK OFF
SELECT 'DROP TABLE ' || table_name || ';'
  FROM user_tables
 WHERE table_name LIKE UPPER ('&1%')

SPOOL drop.cmd
/
SPOOL OFF
@drop.cmd
```

Now, let's move on to PL/SQL-based generation. My team is about to start a large-scale development effort. We will need to perform retrievals of entire rows of data for many different tables, based on their various (but single) primary key columns. I want to do this in a way that conforms to all of our organization's standards (exception handling with logging, use, and encapsulation of the implicit query that offers best performance, etc.). Rather than write a memo to this effect, I build a procedure:

```
CREATE OR REPLACE PROCEDURE genlookup (tab IN VARCHAR2, col IN VARCHAR2)
IS
    l_ltab   VARCHAR2 (100) := LOWER (tab);
    l_lcol   VARCHAR2 (100) := LOWER (col);
BEGIN
    pl ('CREATE OR REPLACE FUNCTION ' || l_ltab || '_row_for (');
    pl ('    ' ||
          l_lcol || '_in IN ' || l_ltab || '.' || l_lcol || '%TYPE)');
    pl ('   RETURN ' || l_ltab || '%ROWTYPE');
    pl ('IS');
    pl ('    retval  ' || l_ltab || '%ROWTYPE;');
    pl ('BEGIN');
    pl ('   SELECT * INTO retval');
    pl ('     FROM ' || l_ltab);
    pl ('    WHERE ' || l_lcol || ' = ' || l_lcol || '_in;');
    pl ('   RETURN retval;');
    pl ('EXCEPTION');
    pl ('   WHEN NO_DATA_FOUND THEN');
    pl ('      RETURN NULL;');
    pl ('   WHEN OTHERS THEN');
    pl ('      err.log;');
    pl ('END ' || l_ltab || '_row_for;');
    pl ('/');
END;
/
```

And I can then use this procedure as follows:

```
SQL> exec genlookup ('book', 'isbn')
CREATE OR REPLACE FUNCTION book_row_for (
    isbn_in IN book.isbn%TYPE)
    RETURN book%ROWTYPE
IS
    retval  book%ROWTYPE;
BEGIN
    SELECT * INTO retval
      FROM book
     WHERE isbn = isbn_in;
    RETURN retval;
EXCEPTION
    WHEN NO_DATA_FOUND THEN
        RETURN NULL;
    WHEN OTHERS THEN
        err.log;
END book_row_for;
/
```

You can get much more sophisticated in your generation efforts; you can, for example, look up the primary key column(s) in the ALL_CONS_COLUMNS data dictionary view, instead of having to specify the WHERE clause column. You have to decide for yourself where to draw the line: do you really need that flexibility or does it just look like lots of fun to build?

## Benefits

You can build your applications faster; utilities can generate software lots faster than you can type it.

You will improve the quality of your application code: assuming that your generator program has been well-designed and tested, it will generate bug-free code with each use.

As your underlying data structures change, you can regenerate program units that work with those data structures. Much less time is spent upgrading existing code.

## Challenges

Building anything but the most crude generators involves a level of abstraction and complexity higher than the usual task tackled by most developers.

## Resources

### Commercial Code-Generation Tools

*http://www.oracle.com*: Oracle Designer from Oracle Corporation generates code in a variety of languages.

*http://www.revealnet.com*: RevealNet's PL/Generator generates comprehensive encapsulation packages for tables and views.

*PLVgen*: RevealNet's Active PL/SQL Knowledge Base offers PLVgen, a package that generates functions, procedures, cursor FOR loops and other code elements. Visit the PL/SQL Pipeline archives as described in the Preface.

Most CASE/designer tools offer some level of code generation. Visit the web sites of Quest, Computer Associates, Precise, BMC, Embarcadero, and so on to check out their respective products.

### Code-Generation Utilities

*genlookup.pro*: Generates a lookup procedure that returns a row in a table.

*msginfo.pkg*: Generates a package with definitions for all application-specific exceptions.

*genmods.pkg*: Generates standard formatted functions.

---

## DEV-06: Set up and use formal unit testing procedures.

A unit test is a test a developer creates to ensure that his or her "unit," usually a single program, works properly. A unit test is very different from a system or functional test; these latter types of tests are oriented to application features or overall testing of the system. You can't properly or effectively perform a system test until you know that the individual programs behave as expected.

So, of course, you would therefore expect that programmers do lots of unit testing and have a correspondingly high level of confidence in their programs. Ah, if only that were the case! The reality is that programmers generally perform an inadequate number of inadequate tests and figure that if the users don't find a bug, there is no bug. Why does this happen? Let me count the ways:

*The psychology of success and failure*
> We are so focused on getting our code to work correctly that we generally shy away from bad news, from even wanting to take the chance of getting bad news. Better to do some cursory testing, confirm that it seems to be working OK, and then wait for others to find bugs, if there are any (as if there were any doubt).

*Deadline pressures*
> Hey, it's Internet time! Time to market determines all. We need everything yesterday, so let's be just like Microsoft and Netscape: release pre-beta software as production and let our users test/suffer through our applications.

*Management's lack of understanding*
> IT management is notorious for not really understanding the software development process. If we aren't given the time and authority to write (write, that is, in the broadest sense, including testing, documentation, refinement, etc.) our own code properly, we will always end up with buggy junk that no one wants to admit ownership of.

*Overhead of setting up and running tests*
> If it's a big deal to write and run tests, they won't get done. I don't have time, and there is always something else to work on. One consequence of this point is that more and more of the testing is handed over to the QA department, if there is one. That transfer of responsibility is, on the one hand, positive. Professional quality assurance professionals can have a tremendous impact on application quality. Yet we developers must take and exercise

responsibility for unit testing our own code, otherwise, the testing/QA process is much more frustrating and extended.

*Ego*

I wrote it; therefore it works the way I intended it to work.

The bottom line is that our code almost universally needs more testing. And the best way to do unit testing is with a formal procedure built around software that makes testing as easy and as automated as possible. I can't help with deadline pressures, and my ability to improve your manager's understanding of the need to take more time to test is limited. I can, on the other hand, offer you a "framework"—a set of processes and code elements—that can greatly improve your ability to perform high quality unit testing.

In the spring of 2000, I studied Extreme Programming (*http://www.xprogramming.com*) and its associated concepts on unit testing (most widely used in its Java interpretation, the open source JUnit). I then adapted these ideas to the world of PL/SQL, creating utPLSQL, the unit testing framework for Oracle PL/SQL.

By the time this book is published, there may be other unit testing facilities available for PL/SQL. As a starting point for exploring the implementation of formal unit tests for your code, however, I encourage you to visit *http://oracle.oreilly.com/utplsql*.

## Example

With utPLSQL, you build a test package for your standalone or packaged programs. You then ask utPLSQL to run the tests in your test package, and display the results. When you use utPLSQL, you don't have to analyze the results and determine whether your tests succeeded or failed; the utility automatically figures that out for you.

Suppose, for example, that I have built a simple alternative to the SUBSTR function called betwnstr: it returns the substring found between the specified start and end locations in the string. Here it is:

```
CREATE OR REPLACE FUNCTION betwnstr (
    string_in IN VARCHAR2,
    start_in IN INTEGER,
    end_in IN INTEGER
    )
    RETURN VARCHAR2
IS
BEGIN
    RETURN (
        SUBSTR (
            string_in,
            start_in,
            end_in - start_in + 1
            )
        );
END betwnstr;
/
```

To test this function, I want to pass in a variety of inputs, as shown in this table:

| String | Start | End | Expected Result |
|---|---|---|---|
| abcdefg | 3 (positive number) | 5 (bigger positive number) | cde |
| abcdefg | NULL | Any | NULL |
| abcdefg | Any | NULL | NULL |
| abcdefg | 5 | 2 (end smaller than start | NULL |
| abcdefg | 3 | 200 (end larger than string length) | cdefg |

From this table (which, of course, doesn't yet cover all the variations needed for a comprehensive test), I build test cases for each entry in my test package's unit test procedure:

```
CREATE OR REPLACE PACKAGE BODY ut_betwnstr
IS
   PROCEDURE ut_betwnstr IS
   BEGIN
      utassert.eq ('Typical valid usage',
         betwnstr (string_in => 'abcdefg', start_in => 3, end_in => 5),
         'cde');

      utassert.isnull ('NULL start',
         betwnstr (string_in=> 'abcdefg',
            start_in    => NULL,
            end_in      => 5));

      utassert.isnull ('NULL end',
         betwnstr (string_in=> 'abcdefg',
            start_in    => 2,
            end_in      => NULL));

      utassert.isnull ('End smaller than start',
         betwnstr (string_in => 'abcdefg', start_in => 5, end_in => 2));

      utassert.eq ('End larger than string length',
         betwnstr (string_in=> 'abcdefg',
            start_in    => 3,
            end_in      => 200),
         'cdefg');

   END ut_betwnstr;
END ut_betwnstr;
/
```

I call the utAssert procedures so that the results of my tests (my "assertions" that such and such is true) can be logged automatically with utPLSQL.

Then I can run the test and view the results. Here is a run that identifies no errors:

```
SQL> exec utplsql.test ('betwnstr')
 .
 >    SSSS   U    U   CCC      CCC    EEEEEEE   SSSS     SSSS
 >   S   S  S U   U C   C   C   C  E         S   S  S    S
 >   S        U   U C      C C     C E       S        S
 >   S        U   U C       C      E       S        S
 >    SSSS   U   U C         C      EEEE    SSSS     SSSS
 >       S  U   U C         C      E           S        S
 >      S U   U C       C C     C E          S         S
 >   S   S  U   U  C   C   C   C  E       S   S  S    S
 >    SSSS    UUU    CCC      CCC    EEEEEEE  SSSS     SSSS
 .
   SUCCESS: "betwnstr"
```

And here is the output shown when problems arise:

```
SQL> exec utplsql.test ('betwnstr')
 .
 >  FFFFFFF    AA      III  L       U       U RRRRR    EEEEEEE
 >  F         A  A     I   L       U       U R    R  E
 >  F        A    A    I   L       U       U R    R E
 >  F        A    A    I   L       U       U R    R E
 >  FFFF    A      A   I   L       U       U RRRRRR  EEEE
 >  F       AAAAAAAA   I   L       U       U R   R   E
 >  F       A      A   I   L       U       U R    R  E
 >  F       A      A   I   L      U   U R    R E
 >  F       A      A  III  LLLLLLL  UUU    R      R EEEEEE
 .
   FAILURE: "betwnstr"
 .
   UT_BETWNSTR: Typical valid usage; expected "cde", got "cd"
   UT_BETWNSTR: IS NULL: NULL start
   UT_BETWNSTR: IS NULL: End smaller than start
```

## Benefits

You develop applications faster, with a higher degree of confidence and with fewer bugs.

It is much easier for other developers to maintain and enhance your code, because after they make a change, they can run the full suite of tests and confirm that the program still passes all tests.

## Challenges

The only challenge to performing comprehensive unit testing is you! You know you have to test your code, and you have to test it repeatedly. So take the time to define your tests within a test package, and use a testing facility to run your tests for you.

Enlist the help of other developers in your organization to review your unit test cases and build others. Did you miss anything? Is your test accurate? It is often difficult for the person who wrote (or is about to write) the code to be objective about it. You'll find more about this topic in **DEV-07**.

### Resources

*http://oracle.oreilly.com/utplsql*: To download utPLSQL and to obtain more information about its approach to unit testing.

*http://www.xprogramming.com*: For more general information about Extreme Programming's approach to and underlying principles for unit testing.

*http://www.extremeprogramming.org*: For a wonderfully accessible, web-based introduction to Extreme Programming.

## DEV-07: Get independent testers for functional sign-off.

Individual developers should and must be responsible for defining and executing unit tests on the programs they write (see **DEV-06**). Developers should not, on the other hand, be responsible for overall functional testing of their applications. There are several reasons for this:

* We don't own the requirements. We don't decide when and if the system works properly. Our users or customers have this responsibility. They need to be intimately connected with, and drive, the functional tests.

* Whenever we test our code, we follow the "pathways to success" without ever knowing it. In other words, the mindset we had when we wrote the code is the same mindset we have when testing the code. Other people, other eyes, need to run the software in complete ignorance of those pathways. It is no wonder that unit testing was so successful and yet integration testing has such problems.

To improve the quality of code that is handed over to customers for testing, your team leader or development manager should:

* Work with the customer to define the set of tests that must be run successfully before an application is considered to be ready for production.

* Establish a distinct testing group—either a devoted Quality Assurance organization or simply a bunch of developers who haven't write any of the software to be tested.

This extra layer of testing, based on the customer's own requirements and performed before the handoff to customers for their "sign off" test, will greatly improve code quality and customer confidence in the development team.

### Example

I spend several days building a really slick application in Oracle Developer (or Visual Basic or Java or…). It allows users to manage data in a few different tables, request reports, and so on. I then devote most of a day to running the application through its paces. I click here, click there, enter good data, enter bad data, find a bunch of bugs, fix them, and finally hand it over to my main customer, Johanna. I feel confident in my application. I can no longer break it.

Imagine how crushed I feel (and I bet you *can* imagine it, because undoubtedly the same thing has happened to you) when Johanna sits down in front of the computer, starts up the application, and in no more than three clicks of the mouse causes an error window to pop up on the screen. The look she sends my way ("Why are you wasting my time?") will stay with me for years.

There is no way for me to convince Johanna that I really, truly did spend hours testing the application. Why should she believe such a thing? She is then left to believe I am a totally incompetent tester.

## Benefits

Quality of code handed to users for testing is higher, which means the end result moved to production is of correspondingly higher quality.

Customer confidence in the development organization remains high. This confidence—and the respect that comes with it—makes it easier for developers to negotiate with customers over the time-versus-quality dilemma so many of us face in software development.

## Challenges

Many small development groups can't afford (i.e., can't convince management to spend the money) to staff a separate QA organization. At a minimum, you must make sure that customers have defined a clear set of tests. Then distribute the functional testing load to the developers so that they do not test their own code.

## Resources

*http://www.well.com/~vision/sqa.html*: A gathering place for references related to the theory and practice of Software Quality Assurance. This site is growing to include information on Standards and Development Procedures, Product Evaluation and Process Monitoring, Configuration Management Monitoring, the role of SQA in the Product Development Cycle, and Automated Testing Tools.

# 2

# *Coding Style and Conventions*

Software developers are a very privileged bunch. We don't have to work in dangerous environments, and our jobs aren't physically taxing (though carpal tunnel syndrome is always a threat). We are paid to think about things, and then to write down our thoughts in the form of code. This code is then used and maintained by others, sometimes for decades.

Given this situation, I believe we all have a responsibility to write code that can be easily understood and maintained (and, c'mon, let's admit our secret desires, admired) by developers who follow in our footsteps.

 Steve McConnell's *http://www.construx.com* site, along with his book, *Code Complete* (Microsoft Press), offers checklists on coding style, naming conventions and rules, and module definitions.

### STYL-01: Adopt a consistent, readable format that is easy to maintain.

Your code should have a "signature," a style that is consistent (all your programs look the same), readable (anyone can pick up your code and make sense of it), and maintainable (a minor change in the code shouldn't require 15 minutes of reformatting).

Ideally, everyone in your organization would adopt a similar style, so that everyone can easily understand everyone else's code. This can be tricky, as programmers sometimes take a dogmatic approach to such issues as size of indentation and use of whitespace.

You have two options regarding coding style:

- Find or write a set of guidelines, and then try as hard as you can to follow (and get your group to follow) those guidelines. See the "Resources" section for a sample document.

- Use a tool to automatically format your code for you. The dominant code formatter for PL/SQL is currently PL/Formatter from RevealNet (see "Resources"). This product is not only available standalone, but is also integrated into many popular integrated development environments (IDEs).

I strongly recommend that you use PL/Formatter or some other "pretty print" tool. It is quite liberating to write code without any concern whatsoever for how it looks: I focus completely on the logical flow and then press a button a moment later to turn it into readable, attractive code.

## Example

Here is a package specification that has some clear problems: all uppercase, no indentation, no whitespace:

```
CREATE OR REPLACE PACKAGE OVERDUE_PKG IS
PROCEDURE SET_DAILY_FINE (FINE_IN IN NUMBER);
FUNCTION DAILY_FINE RETURN NUMBER;
FUNCTION DAYS_OVERDUE
(ISBN_IN IN BOOK.ISBN%TYPE)RETURN INTEGER;
FUNCTION FINE (ISBN_IN IN BOOK.ISBN%TYPE)
RETURN INTEGER;
END OVERDUE_PKG;
/
```

I ran it through PL/Formatter and came up with this:

```
CREATE OR REPLACE PACKAGE overdue_pkg
IS
    PROCEDURE set_daily_fine (fine_in IN NUMBER);

    FUNCTION daily_fine
       RETURN NUMBER;

    FUNCTION days_overdue (
       isbn_in IN book.isbn%TYPE)
       RETURN INTEGER;

    FUNCTION fine (isbn_in IN book.isbn%TYPE)
       RETURN INTEGER;
END overdue_pkg;
/
```

Which of these specifications would you prefer to read and maintain?

## Benefits

Code can be more effectively reviewed, maintained, and enhanced if it's well-formatted and formatted consistently with the rest of your development team.

---

## *Déjà vu Code*

I wrote and enacted a PL/SQL Coding Standard at a former client's. After two years there as a consultant, I moved on to other assignments. A year later, I returned to the previous client. I was tasked with maintaining a particular package. Looking at it, I got a strange sense of déjà vu; the code looked like something I would have written, but I could not remember having written it. Since it was laid out according to the prescribed standard, it was easy to locate sections and make the needed changes. I checked the document header to discover who wrote it, which turned out to be another fellow there. I asked him about it, and he said that he simply followed the standard. He liked how so many packages were all consistently organized, making it a breeze to read and maintain them.

·   —Dan Clamage

---

### Challenges

It's hard to enforce a coding style among programmers, who can be fiercely libertarian.

It takes time to produce a comprehensive style document for PL/SQL.

### Resources

Recommendations for coding style from Chapter 3 of *Oracle PL/SQL Programming*, available online at *http://www.oreilly.com/oracle/oraclep2/*.

*http://www.revealnet.com/products/formatter/formatter.htm*: For information about PL/Formatter.

---

## STYL-02: Adopt logical, consistent naming conventions for modules and data structures.

Adopt and promote standard ways to define names of program elements. Choose a level of "formality" of naming conventions based on your needs. If, for example, you have a team of two developers working on a small code base, you can probably get away with naming conventions that don't go far beyond "use meaningful names." If you are building a massive application involving dozens of developers, you probably need to define more comprehensive rules.

Here are some general recommendations for conventions:

* Identify the scope of a variable in its name. A global variable can be prefaced with g_, for example.

* Use a prefix or suffix to identify the types of structures being defined. Consider, for example, declarations of TYPEs: of collections, objects, records, ref cursors, etc. A standard approach to declaring such a structure is <name>_t. Types are quite different from variables; you should be able to identify the difference with a glance.

- Use the same case convention for user-defined types as the standard datatypes in order to help them stand out. Datatypes (built-in or user-defined) should follow a different casing rule from variables (such as all uppercase for types, lowercase for variables).

- Use a readable format for your names. Since PL/SQL isn't case-sensitive, the "camel notation" (as in minBalanceRequired), for example, is probably not a good choice for constructing names. Instead, use separators such as _ (underscore) to improve readability (as in min_balance_required). While names can be as long as 30 characters, keep them short, as well as readable.

- Organize like items together. For example, declare record variables together in the same section. Declare all constants together in another section, separated from the previous section by whitespace.

It isn't possible to provide a comprehensive list of naming conventions in this book. The particular conventions you choose, furthermore, aren't nearly as important as the fact that you set some standard for naming conventions. See the "Resources" section for downloadable style guides.

## *Example*

Here is a block of code that reflects no standardization of naming conventions:

```
CREATE OR REPLACE PROCEDURE showborrowedbooks (
    date_borrowed IN DATE)
IS
    date_returned DATE := SYSDATE;
    mindaysborrowed INTEGER := 10;

    TYPE book_borrowed IS RECORD (
        dateborrowed DATE,
        daysborrowed INTEGER,
        isbn         book.isbn%TYPE,
        datedue      DATE);

    borrowedbook book_borrowed;

    CURSOR allborrowed IS
        SELECT * FROM borrowed_book
         WHERE returned = 'N';
BEGIN
    IF dateborrowed < datereturned
    THEN
        FOR rec IN allborrowed
        LOOP
            borrowedbook:= rec;

            IF borrowedbook.daysborrowed > mindaysborrowed
            THEN
                pl (borrowedbook.isbn);
            END IF;
        END LOOP;
    END IF;
END showborrowedbooks;
```

Here's that same block of code based on standards. I use underscores in names; suffixes on parameters, records, and cursors; prefixes to show scope (1_ for local) and type (c_ for constant). Compare carefully the following item names with those in the previous example:

```
CREATE OR REPLACE PROCEDURE show_borrowed_books (
    date_borrowed_in IN DATE)
IS
    c_date_returned CONSTANT DATE := SYSDATE;
    l_min_days_borrowed INTEGER := 10;

    TYPE book_borrowed_rt IS RECORD (
        date_borrowed DATE,
        days_borrowed INTEGER,
        isbn          book.isbn%TYPE,
        date_due      DATE);

    borrowed_book_rec book_borrowed_rt;

    CURSOR all_borrowed_cur IS
        SELECT * FROM borrowed_book
         WHERE returned = 'N';
BEGIN
    IF date_borrowed_in < c_date_returned
    THEN
        FOR book_rec IN all_borrowed_cur
        LOOP
            borrowed_book_rec := book_rec;

            IF borrowed_book_rec.days_borrowed >
                l_min_days_borrowed
            THEN
                p1 (borrowed_book_rec.isbn);
            END IF;
        END LOOP;
    END IF;
END show_borrowed_books;
```

Now it's possible to look at any individual part of show_borrowed_books and make sense of the different kinds of structures manipulated by the program.

### Benefits

By setting standards, you don't have to constantly worry about how to write your code. Concentrate on the important stuff: the business logic.

Developers come up to speed more quickly on the code base as they transfer into new groups; they also transfer their knowledge and productivity from one project to another.

### Challenges

Define naming standards that are appropriate to your project (not overly rigid for the size of the team and complexity of the application).

Get developer buy-in for the conventions. One way to achieve this is to get the developers themselves to set those conventions.

Check for compliance with conventions (although this is difficult to do). You can build scripts in PL/SQL and SQL to analyze source code for conformance with *some* rules (e.g., "Don't use fixed-length CHAR declarations."). Currently, a comprehensive review must be performed manually; I hope that tools will become available in the next several years.

### Resources

See Steve McConnell's *http://www.construx.com* site and his *Code Complete* book for naming convention suggestions.

*standards.doc*: An unfinished draft of some naming and coding standards for PL/SQL developers; be sure to review and edit this document before using in your organization.

*standards.zip*: An HTML-driven comprehensive guide to a set of naming conventions for PL/SQL code (courtesy of Matthew MacFarland).

---

## STYL-03: Standardize module and program headers.

While you should generally keep comments to a minimum in your code (see STYL-09), it's extremely important to create and keep current a standard header for all programs. This header should contain, at a minimum, the following elements:

- *Version, author, and copyright information*: What is the version of the code? Who wrote the program, who owns the program, etc.

- *Access information*: Where is the program stored? On disk in a file? Within the database under a certain schema?

- *Overview*: What does this program do?

- *Dependencies*: What does this program need to have defined, or have access to, in order to run properly?

- *Algorithms*: Are any algorithms of special note used in the program? If so, specify them and/or supply a more detailed description of the theory of operation (if there is one).

- *Scope*: What application module(s) was the program written for (if it's not a generic library-type of program)? Frequently, packages are backend components of a system with a complex frontend. For example, a set of packages might comprise the Payroll subsystem.

- *Modification history*: What modifications have been made to the program? Include a line entry for each change to the program, showing who, when, and what. Put the entries in date-descending order, so that the most recent change is at the top.

- *Exceptions*: What errors might be raised by the program?

You are best off defining this header *after* the IS or AS keyword in your program definition. For example:

```
CREATE OR REPLACE PROCEDURE my_procedure
IS
/*
... header text
*/
```

When you put the header inside the program definition, that header is also stored in the USER_SOURCE data dictionary view, making it accessible to analysis.

## Example

Here's a standard header format that follows an XML-like syntax (see the "Resources" section for a package that helps you leverage this standardized format in your development process):

```
/*
<VERSION>1.0.5</VERSION>
<FILENAME>stdhdr.pkg</FILENAME>
<AUTHOR>Steven Feuerstein</AUTHOR>
<SUMMARY>API to standard headers in code</SUMMARY>
<COPYRIGHT>Steven Feuerstein, 2000</COPYRIGHT>

<OVERVIEW>
   Rather than simply document a standard header
   for programs, this package offers a package-based
   API so that you can easily extract information
   stored in the header.
</OVERVIEW>

<DEPENDENCIES>
   ALL_SOURCE data dictionary view
</DEPENDENCIES>

<EXCEPTIONS>None</EXCEPTIONS>

Modification History
Date       By         Modification
---------- ---------  ------------------------------
<MODIFICATIONS>
06/30/2000 SEF        Change to XML-compatible syntax
06/07/2000 SEF        Program created
</MODIFICATIONS>
*/
```

## Benefits

You can, at a glance, grasp all the administrative aspects of the program.

An accurate modification history makes it easier to maintain the code.

The various sections can be parsed and stored anywhere as ongoing documentation (showing the changes the program underwent). This benefit, combined with capturing the last DDL timestamp, makes for good QA of the production database.

## Challenges

If the header isn't kept up to date, it's worse than useless: it's misleading. Most importantly, developers must update the modification history with every change. If the code modifications point back to the version comment in the header, that's even better.

### Resources

*stdhdr.pkg*: A prototype "standard header" package that generates a standard header (with an XML-style format) and offers programs to query such headers from stored code.

## STYL-04: Tag module END statements with module names.

Every program (indeed, every block of code; see **STYL-06**) has an END statement. You can, and should, append the name of the program to the end statement:

```
CREATE OR REPLACE PACKAGE BODY <pkgname>
IS
    PROCEDURE <procname> (...)
    IS BEGIN
        ...
    END <procname>;

    PROCEDURE <funcname> (...)
    IS BEGIN
        ...
    END <funcname>;

END <pkgname>;
```

### Example

My package consists of 243 procedures and functions, stretching to over 5,000 lines. Without END labels, I could easily be confronted with code like this:

```
        END LOOP;
    END;
END;
```

Yikes! Wouldn't it be so much better if my code had instead been written like this:

```
        END LOOP yearly_analysis;
    END best_seller_review;
END book_usage_pkg;
```

### Benefits

This is merely good form for standalone programs. For packaged procedures and functions with code that goes on for hundreds or thousands of lines, however, named ENDs are crucial to improving the readability of that package.

## STYL-05: Name procedures with verb phrases and functions with noun phrases.

We build procedures to join together (and run) a series of logically related executable statements. The name of the procedure should reflect what those statements do, and should be in the form of a verb phrase, as in:

```
PROCEDURE calculate_totals (...);
PROCEDURE display_favorite_flavors (...);
```

A function executes one or more statements with the express intent of returning a value. The name of a function should describe what is being returned and be in the form of a noun phrase, as in:

```
FUNCTION total_salary (...) RETURN NUMBER;
FUNCTION book_title (...) RETURN VARCHAR2;
```

You might also consider standardizing elements of your procedures' verb phrases; standard prefixes can indicate the type of operation. Here are some example:

`ins_`
> Inserts something

`get_`
> Selects something

`del_`
> Deletes something

`upd_`
> Updates something

`chk_`
> Validates something

### Example

The following table shows some *bad* names for procedures and functions:

| Name | What's Wrong? | Better Name |
| --- | --- | --- |
| PROCEDURE total_salary | What is the procedure doing with total salary? Displaying it? Calculating it? | display_ total_salary |
| FUNCTION calculate_ total_salary | Well, of course, you're calculating the total salary—and returning it as well. | total_salary |
| FUNCTION get_total_ salary | What else does a function do but *get* and return things? Use of the get_ prefix is unnecessary; the function usage in code makes this clear. | total_salary |

### Benefits

The more accurately a name reflects the purpose and usage of a program, the easier it is to understand code that uses that program.

### Challenges

Enumerate the kinds of verb and noun phrases you might use repeatedly, and standardize a set of prefixes for them.

## STYL-06: Self-document using block and loop labels.

While PL/SQL labels (identifiers within double angle brackets, such as <<yearly_ analysis>>) are most often associated with GOTOs and are therefore disdained, they can be a big help in improving the readability of code.

Use a label directly in front of loops and nested anonymous blocks:

- To name that portion of code and thereby self-document what it's doing
- So you can repeat that name with the END statement of that block or loop

This recommendation is especially important when you have multiple nestings of loops (and possibly inconsistent indentation), as in the following:

```
LOOP
   <body>
   WHILE <condition>
   LOOP
      <while body>
   END LOOP;
END LOOP;
```

## Example

I use labels for a block and two nested loops, and then apply them in the appropriate END statements. I can now easily see *which* loop and block is ending, no matter how badly my code is indented!

```
CREATE OR REPLACE PROCEDURE display_book_usage
IS
BEGIN
   <<best_seller_review>>
   DECLARE
      CURSOR yearly_analysis_cur IS SELECT ...;
      CURSOR monthly_analysis_cur IS SELECT ...;
   BEGIN
      <<yearly_analysis>>
      FOR book_rec IN yearly_analysis_cur (2000)
      LOOP
         <<monthly_analysis>>
         FOR month_rec IN
            monthly_analysis_cur (
               yearly_analysis_cur%rowcount)
         LOOP
            ... lots of month-related code ...
         END LOOP monthly_analysis;
         ... lots of year-related code ...
      END LOOP yearly_analysis;
   END best_seller_review;
END display_book_usage;
```

## Benefits

If you use labels, it's much easier to read your code, especially if it contains loops and nested blocks that have long bodies (i.e., the loop starts on page 2 and ends on page 7, with three other loops inside that outer loop).

## STYL-07: Express complex expressions unambiguously using parentheses.

The rules of operator precedence follow the commonly accepted precedence of algebraic operators. The strong typing approach of PL/SQL,[*] combined with the common precedence rules, make many parentheses unnecessary. When an uncommon combination of operators occurs, however, it may be helpful to add parentheses even when the precedence rules apply.

The rules of evaluation do specify left-to-right evaluation for operators that have the same precedence level. However, this is the most commonly overlooked rule of evaluation when checking expressions for correctness.

Many developers apply a consistent rule for improved readability in this area: always use parentheses around every Boolean expression, including IF, ELSIF, and WHILE statements, as well as variable assignments, regardless of the simplicity of the expressions. So, rather than:

```
IF cust_rec.min_balance < 1000 THEN ...
```

you instead write:

```
IF ( cust_rec.min_balance < 1000 ) THEN ...
```

### Example

You might not want a standard that requires you to always use parentheses, but in some situations, parentheses are all but required for readability. Consider the following expression:

```
5 + Y**3 MOD 10
```

The PL/SQL compiler will not be the least bit confused by this statement; it will apply its unambiguous rules and come up with an answer. Developers, however, may not have such an easy time of it. You are better off writing that same line of code as follows:

```
5 + ((Y ** 3) MOD 10)
```

### Benefits

Everyone, including the author of the code, can more easily understand the logic and intent (which is crucial for maintenance) of complex expressions.

## STYL-08: Use vertical code alignment to emphasize vertical relationships.

A common code formatting technique is *vertical alignment*. Here is an example in a SQL WHERE clause:

```
WHERE  COM.company_id      = SAL.company_id
   AND COM.company_type_cd = TYP.company_type_cd
```

---

[*] In a strongly typed programming language, you must declare each type of data structure before you can work with it. And when you declare it, you specify its type and, optionally, an initial or default value. Certain operations are allowed only with certain types.

```
AND TYP.company_type_cd = CFG.company_type_cd
AND COM.region_cd       = REG.region_cd
AND REG.status          = RST.status;
```

You should use vertical alignment only when the elements that are lined up vertically have a relationship with each other that you want to express. In the WHERE clause shown here, however, there is no relationship between the right sides of the various expressions. The relationship is between the left and right sides of each individual expression. This is, therefore, a misuse of vertical alignment.

### Example

Developers often (and justifiably) use vertical alignment with program parameter lists, as in:

```
PROCEDURE maximize_profits (
    advertising_budget    IN      NUMBER,
    bribery_budget        IN OUT NUMBER,
    merge_and_purge_on    IN      DATE := SYSDATE,
    obscene_bonus         OUT     NUMBER);
```

Vertical alignment allows you to easily see the different parameter modes and datatypes.

Vertical alignment is also handy when declaring many constants, as in:

```
CREATE OR REPLACE PACKAGE genAPI
IS
    c_table       CONSTANT CHAR(5)   := 'TABLE';
    c_column      CONSTANT CHAR(6)   := 'COLUMN';
    c_genpky      CONSTANT CHAR(6)   := 'GENPKY';
    c_genpkyonly  CONSTANT CHAR(10)  := 'GENPKYONLY';
    c_sequence    CONSTANT CHAR(7)   := 'SEQNAME';
    c_pkygenproc  CONSTANT CHAR(10)  := 'PKYGENPROC';
    c_pkygenfunc  CONSTANT CHAR(10)  := 'PKYGENFUNC';
    c_usingxmn    CONSTANT CHAR(8)   := 'USINGXMN';
    c_fromod2k    CONSTANT CHAR(8)   := 'FROMOD2K';
```

In this case, I want to be able to scan the list of values to make sure they are unique. I can also easily compare lengths of strings with the CHAR declarations, avoiding nuisance VALUE_ERROR exceptions on initialization.

Here are some other code elements for which vertical alignment adds value:

- CREATE TABLE statements that define all the individual columns.

- Record TYPE declarations (they have roughly the same structure as a CREATE TABLE statement).

- Series of assignments to fields of records and other multipart data structures.

### Benefits

Careful and appropriate use of vertical alignment enhances readability. Used inappropriately, however, vertical alignment actually makes it harder to see what is really going on in your code.

### Challenges

Vertical alignment is a "high maintenance" format. Add a new, long variable name, and you find yourself reformatting 20 other lines of code to match. An automatic formatter comes in very handy when you decide to format vertically.

## STYL-09: Comment tersely with value-added information.

The best way to explain what your code is doing is to let that code speak for itself. You can take advantage of many self-documentation techniques, including:

- Define variables and call programs (local modules, in particular; see **MOD-04**) to give names to and hide complex expressions.

- Use the language construct that best reflects the code you are writing (declare CONSTANTS when values don't change, choose the right kind of loop for your logic, etc.).

Whenever you find yourself adding a comment to your code, first consider whether it is possible to modify the code itself to express your comment. Good reasons to add comments include:

- Program headers (see **STYL-03**)

- Explanations of workarounds, patches, operating-system dependencies, and other "exceptional" circumstances

- Complex or opaque logic

### Example

Let's follow a trail of unnecessarily commented code to self-documenting code. I start with:

```
/* If the first field of the properties record is N... */
IF properties_flag.field1 = 'N'
```

Yikes! My line of code was incomprehensible and my comment simply repeated the code using the English language, rather than PL/SQL. No added value, no real assistance, yet not at all uncommon. The least I can do is use the comment to "translate" from computer-talk to business requirement:

```
/* If the customer is not eligible for a discount... */
IF properties_flag.field1 = 'N'
```

That's better, but I have created a redundancy: if my requirement ever changes, I have to change the comment *and* the code. Why not change the names of my variables and literals so that the code explains itself?

```
IF customer_flag.discount = constants.ineligible
```

Much better! Now I no longer need a comment. My remaining concern with this line of code is that it "exposes" a business rule; it shows how (at this moment in time) I determine whether a customer is eligible for a discount. Business rules are notorious for changing over time—and for being referenced in multiple places throughout my application. So my best bet is to hide the rule behind a self-documenting function call:

```
IF NOT customer_rules.eligible_for_discount (customer_id)
```

### Benefits

By emphasizing reliance on code and not comments to explain, your program becomes more concise and more readable.

When business requirements change, you don't have to change the code *and* the comment that explained the code.

The business rule is likely to be reused in many other places in your application (see **MOD-01**).

### Challenges

It can be difficult to recognize formulas and business rules (especially when you have been asked to maintain or modify someone else's programs, or when you are new to an application).

Once you recognize an exposed formula, you have to be careful about extracting it from the code and replacing it with a variable or program call.

---

## STYL-10: Adopt meaningful naming conventions for source files.

This is a "meta-code" style issue. You should define a standard for the way you name the operating system files that contain your source code (some organizations now store and edit source code entirely in the database, but they are still in the minority). These files can contain many different kinds of "code":

- DDL definitions of data structures (tables, indexes, GRANT statements, etc.)
- SQL*Plus scripts that contain a variety of anonymous blocks and standalone SQL statements, as well as SQL*Plus formatting/control commands
- PL/SQL program definitions

You need to be careful of how you organize the code in your files. Otherwise, you will end up with a plethora of files in a mish-mash of subdirectories. Your development team will have a hard time figuring out where anything is, and what all those files are supposed to do.

You should also be deliberate in how you name those files, including their extensions. There is a strong tendency in the Oracle world to use the *.sql* extension for all files. Why? Because *.sql* is the default extension of SQL*Plus: if you don't specify an extension, that tool automatically looks for a *.sql* file. Laziness, however, is a poor excuse for a naming convention; by relying on a single extension, you forego valuable "real estate" in that filename.

Here are some recommendations for file-usage conventions:

- Use separate files for each distinct program or package. Don't jumble a bunch of stuff together in a single file. In particular, put your package specification in a different file from the package body. That way, you can recompile the body without recompiling the specification (the latter action causes all dependent programs to be marked invalid).

- Use filenames that accurately describe the contents of the file. If your file contains the definition of a procedure, use the name of the procedure as the filename.

- Set a standard for file extensions that indicates the type of code inside the file (as shown in the "Examples" section).

## Examples

Here are some suggestions for standard file extensions:

| Contents of File | Extension |
|---|---|
| Package specification | *.pks* |
| Package body | *.pkb* |
| Package specification and body[a] | *.pkg* |
| Procedure | *.pro* (or *.sp* for stored procedure) |
| Function | *.fun* (or *.sf* for stored function) |
| Create table script(s) | *.tab* or *.ddl* |
| Synonym creation statements | *.syn* |
| Index definitions | *.ind* |
| Constraint definitions | *.con* |
| Test script | *.tst* |

[a] This makes sense to do only for small, self-contained packages that don't reference other program units.

## Benefits

The name of the file (including its extension) will "tell a story" about its contents, such as the type of code, the name of the program, etc. This increased transparency makes it easier for all developers to work with and maintain the code.

# 3

# *Variables and Data Structures*

PL/SQL is a *strongly typed* language. This means that before you can work with any kind of data structure, you must first declare it. And when you declare it, you specify its type and, optionally, an initial or default value. All declarations of these variables must be made in the declaration section of your anonymous block, procedure, function, or package.

## *Declaring Variables and Data Structures*

Use the best practices described in this section when you declare your data structures.

### *DAT-01: Match datatypes to computational usage.*

Gee, that's a general best practice, isn't it? Of *course* you should do things the right way. So the question becomes: what datatype is the correct datatype? The following table offers some concrete advice on potential issues you might encounter:

| Datatype | Issues and Recommendations |
|----------|----------------------------|
| NUMBER | If you don't specify a precision, as in NUMBER(12,2), Oracle supports up to 38 digits of precision. If you don't need this precision, you're wasting memory. |
| CHAR | This is a fixed-length character string and is mostly available for compatibility purposes with code written in earlier versions of Oracle. The values assigned to CHAR variables are right-padded with spaces, which can result in unexpected behavior. Avoid CHAR unless it's specifically needed. |

| Datatype | Issues and Recommendations |
|----------|----------------------------|
| VARCHAR | This variation on the VARCHAR2 variable-length declaration is provided by Oracle for compatibility purposes. Eschew VARCHAR in favor of VARCHAR2. |
| VARCHAR2 | The greatest challenge you will run into with VARCHAR2 is to avoid the tendency to hard-code a maximum length, as in VARCHAR2(30). Use %TYPE and SUBTYPE instead, as described later in this chapter.<br>Also, prior to Oracle8, VARCHAR2 variables are treated like variable-length strings for purposes of manipulation and evaluation, but Oracle does allocate the full amount of memory upon declaration. If you declare a variable of VARCHAR2(2000), then Oracle allocates 2000 bytes, even if you use only three. |
| INTEGER | If your integer values fall within the range of $-2^{31}+1$ .. $2^{31}-1$ (a.k.a. $-2147483647$ .. $2147483647$), you should declare your variables as PLS_INTEGER. This is the most efficient format for integer manipulation. |

## DAT-02: Anchor variables to database datatypes using %TYPE and %ROWTYPE.

When you declare a variable using %TYPE or %ROWTYPE, you "anchor" the type of that data to another, previously defined element. If your program variable has the same datatype as (and, as is usually the case, is acting as a container for) a column in a table or view, use %TYPE to define it from that column. If your record has the same structure as a row in a table or view, use %ROWTYPE to define it from that table.

### Example

Here is an example of a "hard-coded" declaration:

```
DECLARE
    l_title VARCHAR2(100);
```

I pretty clearly want to put a book title into this variable. And I checked the data dictionary and found that the title column is defined VARCHAR2(60). So that declaration seemed pretty safe. Unfortunately, two months later, the DBA expanded the column size to VARCHAR2(200)—and a month after that, my code started getting VALUE_ERROR exceptions. Bad news!

A much better approach is shown in the following declaration section:

```
DECLARE
    l_title book.title%TYPE;
```

### Benefits

Your code automatically adapts to underlying changes in data structures. Whenever the data structure against which a declaration is anchored changes, the program containing the anchoring is marked INVALID. Upon recompilation, it automatically uses the new form of the data structure.

These declarations are "self-documenting"; a variable declaration tells anyone who reads it what kind of data this variable is supposed to hold.

### Challenges

You need to know the names of columns in tables. The USER_TAB_COLUMNS data dictionary view contains this information; in SQL*Plus you can use the DESCRIBE command to find this information.

A person reviewing anchored declarations doesn't necessarily know the type of data; he must look up the definition of that column or table in the data dictionary.

## DAT-03: Use SUBTYPE to standardize application-specific datatypes.

The SUBTYPE statement allows you to create "aliases" for existing types of information, in effect creating your own specially named datatypes. Use SUBTYPE when you want to standardize on a set of named datatypes that aren't anchorable back to the database.

### Example

Suppose that my book table has a page_count column, defined as INTEGER(4). I then write a program that calculates the total number of pages I have written across all books. If I declare a variable to hold this value as:

```
DECLARE
    l_total book.page_count%TYPE;
```

I could run into problems. My total count might exceed four digits. In fact, I may well not have any database column I can use for anchoring in this case. Yet, I still should not hard-code a declaration like this:

```
DECLARE
    l_total INTEGER(10);
```

Instead, I will create a package and define a variable there that is big enough to hold the total count:

```
CREATE OR REPLACE PACKAGE book_data
IS
    SUBTYPE total_count_t IS INTEGER (10);
```

and then use that in my declaration section:

```
DECLARE
    l_total book_data.total_count_t;
```

 If you use Oracle7 or Oracle8, the SUBTYPE statement just shown will fail; Oracle doesn't recognize constrained SUBTYPEs until Oracle8*i*. In this case, you can do the following:

```
CREATE OR REPLACE PACKAGE book_data
IS
  total_count INTEGER(10);
  SUBTYPE total_count_t IS total_count;
```

*Benefits*

You standardize or "normalize" all datatype definitions. In other words, any definition appears only once in your application. Everything is anchored from that.

*Challenges*

You will either need to take the time to build a single "datatypes" package containing these definitions, or need to remember to place your standard definitions in the appropriate packages in your application.

## DAT-04: Do not hard-code VARCHAR2 lengths.

Sure, in general, you shouldn't hard-code your datatypes; instead, you should rely on anchoring (see **DAT-02**) and SUBTYPEs (see **DAT-03**). This best practice is a special-case emphasis of those other best practices.

Don't hard-code VARCHAR2 lengths, like:

```
DECLARE
    -- Gee, should be big enough
    big_string VARCHAR2(2000);
```

Such a declaration may seem like a big-enough string, but it's also a ticking time bomb in your application. Either %TYPE back to a database column, or define SUBTYPEs in a package specification that give names to standard VARCHAR2 usages.

*Example*

The basic problem with hard-coding a VARCHAR2 length is that stuff changes. Consider the maximum length possible for a VARCHAR2 column in the database. It was 2000 up through Oracle8, and then it expanded to 4000 in Oracle8*i*. The best way to handle this situation is to create a special type:

```
CREATE OR REPLACE app_types
IS
    SUBTYPE dbmax_vc2 IS VARCHAR2(2000);
```

Then, when you upgrade to Oracle8*i*, you simply change the definition of the SUBTYPE. All usages of that type stay the same.

*Benefits*

Your code is less likely to raise VALUE_ERROR exceptions over time.

## DAT-05: Use CONSTANT declarations for variables whose values do not change.

If you know that the value of your variable isn't going to change, take the time, and make the effort, to declare it as a constant.

*Example*

The following script runs during business hours (9 A.M. to 6 P.M.) and is used to analyze book checkouts in the MYSTERY category:

```
DECLARE
   c_date CONSTANT DATE := TRUNC (SYSDATE);
   c_category CONSTANT book.category%TYPE :=
      'MYSTERY';
BEGIN
   checkouts.analyze (c_date, c_category);
   ...
   -- 75 lines later
   FOR rec IN (
      SELECT * FROM book
      WHERE category = c_category)
   LOOP
      ...
   END LOOP;
```

After writing, testing, and deploying this script, I can be confident that a developer won't, six months from now, make a change to the c_category structure between the call to checkouts.analyze and the FOR loop.

### Benefits

Your code self-documents the usage of this data structure: it should not and cannot change.

A developer can't later mistakenly change the data structure's value.

---

## DAT-06: Perform complex variable initialization in the executable section.

The exception section of a block can trap only errors raised in the executable section of that block. So if the code you run to assign a default value to a variable fails in the declaration section, that error is propagated unhandled out to the enclosing program. It's difficult to debug these problems, so, you must either:

* Be sure that initialization logic doesn't raise an error.

* Perform your initialization at the beginning of the executable section, preferably in a separate "init" program.

### Example

Here's some dangerous code, since it isn't at all apparent what these functions do and what they pass back:

```
CREATE OR REPLACE PROCEDURE find_bestsellers
IS
   l_last_title book.title%TYPE :=
      last_search (SYSDATE);

   l_min_count INTEGER(3) :=
      bestseller.limits (bestseller.low);
BEGIN
```

And here is a much safer approach:

```
CREATE OR REPLACE PROCEDURE find_bestsellers
IS
```

```
l_last_title book.title%TYPE;
l_min_count INTEGER(3);

PROCEDURE init IS
BEGIN
   l_last_title:= last_search (SYSDATE);
   l_min_count:=
      bestseller.limits (bestseller.low);
EXCEPTION
   -- Trap and handle all errors
   -- inside the program
END;
BEGIN
   init;
```

### Benefits

Your programs will behave more reliably; if an error does occur as you initialize variables, you can trap the error locally and decide how you want to handle the situation.

# Using Variables and Data Structures

Use the best practices described in this section when you reference the data structures you have declared in your programs.

---

### DAT-07: Replace complex expressions with Boolean variables and functions.

A Boolean expression evaluates to one of three values: TRUE, FALSE, or NULL. You can use Boolean variables and functions to hide complex expressions; the result is code that is virtually as readable as "straight" English—or whatever language you use to communicate with other human beings.

### Example

```
IF total_sal BETWEEN 10000 AND 50000 AND
   emp_status (emp_rec.empno) = 'N' AND
   (MONTHS_BETWEEN
      (emp_rec.hiredate, SYSDATE) > 10)
THEN
   give_raise (emp_rec.empno);
END IF;
```

Wow, that's hard to understand! It'd be much easier if the code looked like this:

```
IF eligible_for_raise (totsal, emp_rec)
THEN
   give_raise (emp_rec.empno);
END IF;
```

And even if you don't want to (or need to) bother with creating a separate function, you can still move the complexity to a local variable, as in:

```
DECLARE
   eligible_for_raise BOOLEAN :=
      total_sal BETWEEN 10000 AND 50000 AND
         emp_status (emp_rec.empno) = 'N' AND
         (MONTHS_BETWEEN
            (emp_rec.hiredate, SYSDATE) > 10);
BEGIN
   IF eligible_for_raise
   THEN
      give_raise (emp_rec.empno);
   END IF;
```

### Benefits

It will be much easier for anyone to read your code; you can literally *read* it. If you then need to understand how the Boolean expression is computed, you can look "under the covers."

This is a technique that can be applied (with care) to existing "spaghetti code." As you go into a program to fix or enhance it, look for opportunities to simplify and shorten executable sections by shifting complexity to local variables and programs.

### Challenges

Before you modify existing code, make sure you have solid unit test scripts in place so you can quickly verify that your changes haven't introduced bugs into the program.

### Resources

*http://oracle.oreilly.com/utplsql*: utPLSQL, a unit test framework for PL/SQL developers.

---

## DAT-08: Do not overload data structure usage.

This is just one entry of a more general category: "don't be lazy!" When you declare a variable, you should give it a name that accurately reflects its purpose in a program. If you then use that variable in more than one way ("recycling"), you create confusion and, very possibly, introduce bugs.

The solution is to declare and manipulate separate data structures for each distinct requirement.

And here's a general piece of advice: reliance on a "time-saver" short-cut should raise a red flag. You're probably doing (or avoiding) something now for which you will pay later.

### Example

I have a few different needs for an integer value, so I will declare one and use it throughout:

```
DECLARE
   ... other declarations

   intval INTEGER;
BEGIN
```

```
intval := list_of_books.COUNT;

IF intval > 0
THEN
    intval := list_of_books(list_of_books.FIRST).page_count;

    analyze_book (intval);
END IF;
```

It's pretty much impossible to look at any usage of intval and understand what is going on. You have to go back to the most recent assignment. Compare that to the following:

```
DECLARE
    ... other declarations

    l_book_count INTEGER;
    l_page_count INTEGER;
BEGIN
    l_book_count := list_of_books.COUNT;

    IF l_book_count > 0
    THEN
        l_page_count:= list_of_books(list_of_books.FIRST).page_count;

        analyze_book (l_page_count);
    END IF;
```

### Benefits

It's a whole lot easier to understand what your code does.

You can make a change to one variable's usage without worrying about its ripple effect to other areas of your code.

---

## DAT-09: Remove unused variables and code.

You should go through your programs and remove any part of your code that is no longer used. This is a relatively straightforward process for variables and named constants. Simply execute searches for a variable's name in that variable's scope. If you find that the only place it appears is in its declaration, delete the declaration and, by doing so, delete one more potential question mark from your code.

There's never a better time to review all the steps you took, and to understand the reasons you took them, than immediately upon completion of your program. If you wait, you will find it particularly difficult to remember those parts of the program that were needed at one point, but were rendered unnecessary in the end. "Dead zones" in your code become sources of deep insecurity for mainte-nance programmers.

You should also leverage tools that will perform this analysis for you, such as RevealNet's PL/Formatter.

## Example

The following block of code has several dead zones that could cause a variety of problems. Can you find them all?

```
CREATE OR REPLACE PROCEDURE weekly_check (
    isbn_in IN book.isbn%TYPE,
    author_in IN VARCHAR2)
IS
    l_count PLS_INTEGER;
    l_counter PLS_INTEGER;
    l_available BOOLEAN;
    l_new_location PLS_INTEGER := 1056;
    l_published_date DATE := SYSDATE;
BEGIN
    l_published_date := te_book.published_date (isbn_in);

    IF ADD_MONTHS (SYSDATE, -60) > l_published_date
    THEN
        review_usage;
    ELSIF ADD_MONTHS (SYSDATE, -24) > l_published_date
    THEN
        check_availability (isbn_in, l_available, l_count);

        IF     l_available
            AND /* Turn off due to Req A12.6 */ FALSE
        THEN
            transfer_book (isbn_in, l_count - 1, l_new_location);
        END IF;
    -- Check for reserves
    -- reserve_pkg.analyze_requests (isbn_in);
    END IF;
END;
```

Here's what I found:

- The author_in parameter is declared but never used. It doesn't even have a default value, so you have to pass in an ignored value.
- l_counter is declared but not used.
- l_published_date is assigned a default value of SYSDATE, which is immediately overridden by the call to te_book.published_date.
- The call to transfer_book has been turned off with the addition of AND FALSE.
- The call to reserve_pkg.analyze_requests has been commented out.

## Benefits

It's much easier to maintain, debug and enhance code that doesn't have "dead zones."

## Challenges

There are sometimes valid reasons for keeping dead code in place. You may want to turn off code temporarily. Also, you may need to comment out some logic but still show that this action was done and why. In such cases, make sure that you include the necessary documentation in the code. Even better, use problem tracking or bug reporting software to keep a comprehensive history of any changes made to code.

## DAT-10: Clean up data structures when your program terminates (successfully or with an error).

PL/SQL does an awful lot of cleanup for you, but there are many scenarios in which it's absolutely crucial for you to take your own cleanup actions.

The best way to do this is to standardize on a local cleanup procedure that is to be included in each program. Call this program both at the end of the executable section and in each exception handler WHEN clause.

### Example

The following program manipulates a packaged cursor, declares a DBMS_SQL cursor, and writes information to a file:

```
CREATE OR REPLACE PROCEDURE busy_busy
IS
    fileid UTL_FILE.file_type;
    dyncur PLS_INTEGER;
BEGIN
    dyncur := DBMS_SQL.open_cursor;
    OPEN book_pkg.all_books_by ('FEUERSTEIN');
    fileid := UTL_FILE.fopen (
        '/apps/library', 'bestsellers.txt', 'R');
    ...
EXCEPTION
    WHEN NO_DATA_FOUND
    THEN
        err.log;
        RAISE;
END;
```

If I'm not careful, I can end up with an unclosable dynamic SQL cursor, a still-open packaged cursor that causes an "ORA-06511: PL/SQL: cursor already open" error, and a file that can't be closed without a call to UTL_FILE.FCLOSE_ALL or a disconnect. Here's a much better approach:

```
CREATE OR REPLACE PROCEDURE busy_busy
IS
    fileid UTL_FILE.file_type;
    dyncur PLS_INTEGER;

    PROCEDURE cleanup IS
    BEGIN
        IF book_pkg.all_books_by%ISOPEN
        THEN
            CLOSE book_pkg.all_books_by;
        END IF;

        DBMS_SQL.CLOSE_CURSOR (dyncur);
```

```
            UTL_FILE.FCLOSE (fileid);
         END;
   BEGIN
      dyncur := DBMS_SQL.open_cursor;
      OPEN book_pkg.all_books_by ('FEUERSTEIN');
      fileid := UTL_FILE.fopen (
         '/apps/library', 'bestsellers.txt', 'R');
      ...
      cleanup;
   EXCEPTION
      WHEN NO_DATA_FOUND
      THEN
         err.log;
         cleanup;
         RAISE;
   END;
```

### Benefits

Your programs are less likely to have memory leaks (open cursors) and to cause problems in other programs by leaving data structures in an uncertain state.

By defining a standard cleanup procedure, future developers can easily add new cleanup operations in one place and be certain they will be run at all exit points.

### Challenges

Set up a standard format for your programs, including initialization and cleanup procedures. It's then a challenge to make sure developers use that template.

## DAT-11: Beware of and avoid implicit datatype conversions.

Sometimes, PL/SQL makes life just *too* darn easy for us developers. It will, for example, allow you to write and execute code like this:

```
DECLARE
   my_birthdate DATE := '09-SEP-58';
```

In this case, the runtime engine automatically converts the string to a date, using the default format mask.

You should, however, avoid implicit conversions in your code. There are at least two big problems with relying on PL/SQL to convert data on your behalf:

- Conversion behavior can be non-intuitive. PL/SQL may convert data in ways that you don't expect, resulting in problems, especially within SQL statements.

- Conversion rules aren't under the control of the developer. These rules can change with an upgrade to a new version of Oracle or by changing RDBMS-wide parameters, such as NLS_DATE_FORMAT.

You can convert explicitly using any of the following built-in functions: TO_DATE, TO_CHAR, TO_NUMBER, and CAST.

### Example

The declaration of the my_birthdate variable is a sterling example of the drawbacks of implicit conversion.

```
DECLARE
    my_birthdate DATE := '09-SEP-58';
```

This code raises an error if the default format mask for the instance is anything but DD-MON-YY or DD-MON-RR. That format is set (and changed) in the parameter initialization file—well out of the control of most PL/SQL developers. It can also be modified for a specific session. A much better approach is:

```
DECLARE
    my_birthdate DATE :=
        TO_DATE ('09-SEP-58', 'DD-MON-RR');
```

### Benefits

The behavior of your code is more consistent and predictable, since you aren't relying on something external to your code. Explicit conversions, for example, would have avoided the vast majority of Y2K issues in PL/SQL code.

### Resources

*bool.pkg*: A package to convert between Booleans and strings, since Oracle doesn't offer any built-in utilities to do this.

# Declaring and Using Package Variables

Use the best practices described in this section when you are declaring variables for use in packages.

## DAT-12: Package application-named literal constants together.

Never place a hard-coded literal, such as "Y" or 150 in your code. Instead, create a package to hold these values and publish a name to be used in place of the literals. You will probably find it best to:

- Define constants that are referenced throughout your application in a single, central package.

- Define constants that are more specific to a single area of functionality within the package that encapsulates that functionality.

### Example

Here is a portion of a general constants package:

```
CREATE OR REPLACE PACKAGE constants
IS
    -- Standard string representation of TRUE/FALSE
    tval CONSTANT CHAR(1) := 'T';
    fval CONSTANT CHAR(1) := 'F';

    -- Earliest valid date: 5 years past
    min_date CONSTANT DATE :=
        ADD_MONTHS (SYSDATE, -5 * 12);
```

And here is a package that contains constants specific to one area of functionality:

```
CREATE OR REPLACE PACKAGE nightly_transform
IS
    c_max_weeks CONSTANT INTEGER := 54;

    c_active CONSTANT CHAR(1) := 'A';
    c_inactive CONSTANT CHAR(1) := 'I';

    c_english CONSTANT INTEGER := 1;
    c_usa CONSTANT INTEGER := 1;
    c_namerica CONSTANT VARCHAR2(2) := 'N';
END nightly_transform;
```

### Benefits

You're less likely to hard-code literal values in your programs, thus improving the readability and maintainability of your code.

Youve established a place to go when a developer needs to add another constant to hide a literal.

### Challenges

The entire development team needs to know about the packages and use the constants that have been defined for them.

Be careful about the values you assign to your constants. With cut-and-paste, it's easy to end up assigning a value that's too long and raises the "ORA-06502: PL/SQL: numeric or value error" at runtime—when the package is initialized.

## DAT-13: Centralize TYPE definitions in package specifications.

As you use more and more of the PL/SQL language features, you will define many TYPEs of things, including:

- SUBTYPEs that define application-specific datatypes
- Collection TYPEs, such as lists of numbers, dates, or records
- Referenced cursor TYPEs, from which cursor variables are declared

Some of these TYPEs can be used unchanged throughout your application (there is only one way, for example, to declare an index-by table of dates); other types are specific to some part of an application but are standard within that.

In either case, create a package to hold these standard TYPEs, so that they can be used in multiple programs.

### Example

Here is a portion of a package specification that contains standard TYPE statements for nested and index-by tables:

```
CREATE OR REPLACE PACKAGE colltype
IS
    TYPE boolean_ntab IS TABLE OF BOOLEAN;
```

```
TYPE boolean_ibtab IS TABLE OF BOOLEAN
  INDEX BY BINARY_INTEGER;

TYPE date_ntab IS TABLE OF DATE;

TYPE date_ibtab IS TABLE OF DATE
  INDEX BY BINARY_INTEGER;
  ...
END colltype;
```

### Benefits

Developers write their code more rapidly and with fewer bugs by relying on predefined TYPEs.

As you need to maintain your TYPEs (those based on application-specific elements are, after all, very likely to change), you go to one package and make the change in one place.

### Challenges

Developers must be disciplined enough to seek out predefined TYPEs or to add new TYPEs to existing packages.

### Resources

*colltype.pks*: A package specification of standard collection TYPE definitions.

---

## DAT-14: Use package globals judiciously and only in package bodies.

A *global variable* is a data structure that can be referenced outside the scope or block in which it's declared. In the following block, for example, the l_publish_date is global to the local display_book_info procedure:

```
DECLARE
  l_publish_date DATE;
  ...
  PROCEDURE display_book_info IS
  BEGIN
    DBMS_OUTPUT.PUT_LINE (l_publish_date);
  END;
```

Globals are dangerous and should be avoided, because they create hidden "dependencies" or side-effects. A global doesn't have to be passed through the parameter list, so it's hard for you to even know that a global is referenced in a program without looking at the implementation.

Globals are most often defined in packages. If you declare a variable at the package level (not within any specific program), that variable exists and retains its value for the duration of your session.

The general solution to this problem is to pass the global as a *parameter* in your procedure and function; don't reference it directly within the program. Another general technique to keep in mind is to declare variables, cursors, functions, and other objects as "deeply" as possible (i.e., in the block nearest to where, or within which, that object will be used), in order to reduce the chance of unintended use by other sections of the code.

 Reliance on global data structures can be a particularly acute problem in Oracle Developer's Formsbuilder (previously known as Oracle Forms). Developers have historically relied on (and overused) :GLOBAL data structures to pass information between forms. In the latest versions of Oracle Developer, avoid :GLOBAL variables. Instead, build and share packages (and variables declared within those packages) among forms.

## Example

Here is an example of a function with a hidden dependency on a global variable:

```
CREATE OR REPLACE FUNCTION overdue_fine (
    isbn_in IN book.isbn%TYPE)
    RETURN NUMBER
IS
    l_days_overdue NUMBER;
BEGIN
    l_days_overdue :=
        overdue_pkg.days_overdue (isbn_in, SYSDATE);
    RETURN
        (l_days_overdue * overdue_pkg.g_daily_fine);
END;
```

The global is the amount of the daily fine. It's buried inside the function. By writing the function this way, two things happen: (a) you lose flexibility to pass in a different daily fine amount, as may be required, and (b) if the daily fine has not been set within the overdue package, the function doesn't work properly.

You can get rid of the dependency by adding a parameter:

```
CREATE OR REPLACE FUNCTION overdue_fine (
    isbn_in IN book.isbn%TYPE,
    daily_fine_in IN NUMBER)
    RETURN NUMBER
IS
    l_days_overdue NUMBER;
BEGIN
    l_days_overdue :=
        overdue_pkg.days_overdue (isbn_in, SYSDATE);
    RETURN
        (l_days_overdue * daily_fine_in);
END;
```

## Benefits

By reducing the interdependencies between programs, you can more easily and confidently make a change to one without worrying about the others being affected.

## Challenges

You may need to revamp existing programs to pull out global references and replace them with either parameters or calls to "get and set" programs that encapsulate the global data (see **DAT-15**).

## DAT-15: Expose package globals using "get and set" modules.

Data structures (scalar variables, collections, cursors) declared in the package specification (not within any specific program) are directly referenceable from any program run from a session with EXECUTE authority on the package. This is always a bad idea and should be avoided.

Instead, declare all package-level data in the package body and provide "get and set" programs—a function to GET the value and a procedure to SET the value—in the package specification. Developers can then access the data through these programs, and automatically follow whatever rules you establish for manipulating that data.

### Example

I've created a package to calculate overdue fines. The fine is, by default, $.10 per day, but it can be changed according to this rule: the fine can never be less than $.05 or more than $.25 per day. Here's my first version:

```
CREATE OR REPLACE PACKAGE overdue_pkg
IS
    g_daily_fine NUMBER := .10;

    FUNCTION days_overdue (isbn_in IN book.isbn%TYPE)
        RETURN INTEGER;

    -- Relies on g_daily_fine for calculation
    FUNCTION fine (isbn_in IN book.isbn%TYPE)
        RETURN INTEGER;
END overdue_pkg;
```

You can easily see the problem with this package in the following block:

```
BEGIN
    overdue_pkg.g_daily_fine := .50;

    p1 ('Your overdue fine is ' ||
        overdue_pkg.fine (' 1-56592-375-8'));
END;
```

As you can see, I bypassed the business rule and applied a daily fine of $.50! By "publishing" the daily fine variable, I lost control of my data structure and the ability to enforce my business rules.

The following rewrite of *overdue_pkg* fixes the problem; for the sake of the trees, I show only the replacement of the g_daily_fine variable with its "get and set" programs:

```
CREATE OR REPLACE PACKAGE overdue_pkg
IS
```

```
PROCEDURE set_daily_fine (fine_in IN NUMBER);
PROCEDURE daily_fine RETURN NUMBER;
```

and the implementation:

```
CREATE OR REPLACE PACKAGE BODY overdue_pkg
IS
    g_daily_fine NUMBER := .10;

    PROCEDURE set_daily_fine (fine_in IN NUMBER)
    IS
    BEGIN
        g_daily_fine :=
            GREATEST (LEAST (fine_in, .25), .05);
    END;

    FUNCTION daily_fine
        RETURN NUMBER
    IS
    BEGIN
        RETURN g_daily_fine;
    END;
```

Now it's impossible to bypass the business rule for the daily fine.

 You will be even better off, of course, if you put your maximum and minimum fine information in a database table. Then you can use the package initialization section to load these limits into package data structures. This way, if (when) the data points change, you don't have to change the program itself, just some rows and columns in a table.

### Benefits

The only way to change a value is through the set procedure. The values of your data structures are protected; business rules can be enforced without exception.

You can track all accesses to your data structure—that is, you can put a "watch" on a variable. This is a debugging feature that isn't even supported by Oracle's debugger API (as of Oracle8*i*).

By hiding the data structure, you give yourself the freedom to change how that data is defined without affecting all accesses to the data.

Package data can now be accessed from Oracle Developer tools, such as Formsbuilder. You may not, from "client-side" PL/SQL (i.e., code written in Oracle Developer components) reference stored package elements unless they are procedures or functions.

### Challenges

You need to write get and set programs for your data structures (see the "Resources" section for help in this matter).

Review existing packages to identify data structures defined in specifications—and then fix them by moving the structures to the bodies. You will have to rewrite some existing programs that reference that data, but it will be worth it.

### Resources

*overdue.pkg*: The overdue package.

*PLVgen*: The PLVgen package of PL/Vision generates "get and set" code for any scalar variable; this way you won't have to write the logic again and again.

*p_and_l.pkg* and *watch.pkg*: Demonstration of "watching" a variable.

# 4

# *Control Structures*

Oracle PL/SQL offers a range of constructs that allow you to control the flow of processing, including:

- For conditional logic: the IF statement
- For loop processing: FOR, WHILE, and simple loops
- For branching logic: the GOTO statement

These constructs are relatively straightforward in syntax and usage. There remain, however, several best practices you should take into account when you work with these kinds of statements.

## *Conditional and Boolean Logic*

Follow the best practices in this section when you are using PL/SQL's IF statements.

### *CTL-01: Use ELSIF with mutually exclusive clauses.*

When you need to write conditional logic that has several mutually exclusive clauses (in other words, if one clause is TRUE, no other clause evaluates to TRUE), use the ELSIF construct:

```
IF condA THEN
   ...
ELSIF condB THEN
   ...
ELSIF condN THEN
   ...
```

```
ELSE
    ...
END IF;
```

## Example

At first glance, the following procedure makes sense, but on closer examination, it's a mess:

```
PROCEDURE process_lineitem (line_in IN INTEGER)
IS
BEGIN
    IF line_in = 1
    THEN
        process_line1;
    END IF;
    IF line_in = 2
    THEN
        process_line2;
    END IF;
    ...
    IF line_in = 2045
    THEN
        process_line2045;
    END IF;
END;
```

Every IF statement is executed and each condition evaluated. You should rewrite such logic as follows:

```
PROCEDURE process_lineitem (line_in IN INTEGER)
IS
BEGIN
    IF line_in = 1
    THEN
        process_line1;
    ELSIF line_in = 2
    THEN
        process_line2;
    ...
    ELSIF line_in = 2045
    THEN
        process_line2045;
    END IF;
END;
```

## Benefits

This structure clearly expresses the underlying "reality" of your business logic: if one condition is TRUE, no others can be TRUE.

ELSIF offers the most efficient implementation for processing mutually exclusive clauses. When one clause evaluates to TRUE, all subsequent clauses are ignored.

## *CTL-02: Use IF...ELSIF only to test a single, simple condition.*

The real world is very complicated; the software we write is supposed to map those complexities into applications. The result is that we often end up needing to deal with convoluted logical expressions.

You should write your IF statements in such a way as to keep them as straightforward and understandable as possible. For example, expressions are often more readable and understandable when they are stated in a positive form. Consequently, you are probably better off avoiding the NOT operator in conditional expressions.

### *Example*

It's not at all uncommon to write or maintain code that's structured like this:

```
IF condA AND NOT ( condB OR condC )
THEN
    proc1;
ELSIF condA AND (condB OR condC)
THEN
    proc2;
ELSIF NOT condA AND condD
THEN
    proc3;
END IF;
```

It's also fairly common to get a headache trying to make sense of all of that. You can often reduce the trauma of headache by trading off the simplicity of the IF statement itself (one level of IF and ELSIF conditions) for the simplicity of clauses within multiple levels:

```
IF condA
THEN
    IF (condB OR condC)
    THEN
        proc2;
    ELSE
        proc1;
    END IF;
ELSIF condD
THEN
    proc3
END IF;
```

Don't forget, by the way, to take into account the possibility of your expressions evaluating to NULL. This can throw a monkey wrench into your conditional processing.

### *Benefits*

Following this best practice will make your code easier to read and maintain.

Breaking an expression into smaller pieces can aid maintainability; if and when the logic changes, you can change one IF clause without affecting the logic of others.

## An Exception to the Rule

A notable exception to this best practice is when you need to negate a large AND expression in order to find out efficiently whether one value out of a group is different. For example, I recently needed to test the counts of 10 parallel index-by tables, to see if even one of them was different; if so, it was an error. Because AND expressions short-circuit on FALSE (whereas ORs short-circuit on TRUE), this was more efficient than using a group of ORs. Moreover, the logic read more naturally. For example:

```
IF NOT (arr1.count = arr2.count
   AND arr1.count = arr3.count
   AND arr1.count = arr4.count AND . . .
   AND arr1.count = arr10.count)
   THEN RAISE e_missing_value;
```

—Dan Clamage

### Challenges

Multiple levels of nested IF statements can also decrease readability. You need to strive for a workable balance.

There's a tradeoff between efficiency (fewer conditional statements) and ease of comprehension. "Many times," wrote one reviewer, "I'll code an IF or ELSE with a NULL statement, either to make the code easier to read, or as a placeholder for future logic. However, I may then find myself repeating logic (such as code that resets a variable) under multiple ELSE blocks because I've broken up the IF expression into smaller pieces."

## CTL-03: Replace and simplify IF statements with Boolean expressions.

Sometimes, you will write or come across conditional statements that, while valid, are unnecessary and cumbersome. Such statements often reflect a lack of under-standing about how you can and should use Boolean expressions and variables.

In general, if you see or write code like this:

```
DECLARE
   boolean_variable BOOLEAN;
BEGIN
   IF boolean_variable = TRUE
   THEN
      ...
   ELSIF boolean_variable = FALSE
   THEN
      ...
   END IF;
```

change it to simpler, more direct code:

```
DECLARE
    boolean_variable BOOLEAN;
BEGIN
    IF boolean_variable
    THEN
        ...
    ELSIF NOT boolean_variable
    THEN
        ...
    END IF;
```

### Example

In some cases, you can completely remove an IF statement. Consider the following conditional statement:

```
IF hiredate < SYSDATE
THEN
    date_in_past := TRUE;
ELSE
    date_in_past := FALSE;
END IF;
```

If you've already validated that hiredate can't be or isn't NULL, you can replace the entire IF statement with this single assignment:

```
date_in_past := hiredate < SYSDATE;
```

If hiredate can be NULL, the following statement offers a comparable expression:

```
date_in_past := NVL (hiredate < SYSDATE, FALSE);
```

### Benefits

Following this best practice will make your code more readable and expressive.

# Loop Processing

Follow the best practices in this section when you are using PL/SQL's looping statements.

## CTL-04: Never EXIT or RETURN from WHILE and FOR loops.

The WHILE and FOR loops include "boundary conditions" that determine:

* When and if a loop should execute at all
* When a loop should stop executing

If you use the EXIT or RETURN statements inside a WHILE or FOR loop, you cause an unstructured termination from the loop. The resulting code is hard to trace and debug.

### Example

Here's the bottom half of a function that scans the contents of a collection and returns the row in which a match is found.

```
l_count := titles.COUNT;
FOR indx IN 1 .. l_rowcount
LOOP
    IF l_match_against = titles(indx)
    THEN
        RETURN indx;
    END IF;
END LOOP;

RAISE Exit_Function;
EXCEPTION
    WHEN Exit_Function THEN RETURN NULL;
END;
```

Now this is some *nasty* code. You manage to get all the way down to the end of the executable section, and you are *punished* with an exception! See **MOD-07** for how this violates best practice for a "funnel-shaped" function.

Of course, you're not supposed to get to the end of the function. Instead, the function finds a match and zooms straight out of the function with a RETURN.

Now imagine a function whose body is 200 lines long with nested loops and several different RETURNs in different parts of the loop. Chaos!

### Benefits

By following the maxim "one way in and one way out" for your loops, the resulting code is much easier to understand and debug. If your loop needs to execute at least once (like a Pascal REPEAT statement), you're better off using a simple LOOP construct and testing for the exit condition with EXIT WHEN.

### Challenges

Your exit test in the WHILE expression can become a bit more complex, especially when you have to replace a natural FOR loop with a more mechanical WHILE loop. For example, you have a FOR loop expression that iterates over nested_table.FIRST to nested_table.LAST, but you need to terminate the loop when you find a matching entry. In order to put the exit test in the iteration scheme, you have to now use a WHILE loop, initialize and maintain a loop control variable yourself (for the current offset), and test for the exit condition in the WHILE expression.

---

## CTL-05: Use a single EXIT in simple loops.

This best practice is another variation on "one way in, one way out." It suggests that, whenever possible, you consolidate all exit logic in your simple loop to a single EXIT (or EXIT WHEN) statement.

In general, use the EXIT WHEN statement in place of code like this:

```
IF <> THEN EXIT; END IF;
```

because it's more intuitive and requires less typing.

### Example

Here's part of a program that compares two files for equality. After reading the next line from each file, it checks for the following conditions:

Did I reach the end of both files?
Are the lines different?
Did I reach the end of just one file?

In each case, set the "return value" for the function and also issue an EXIT statement:

```
LOOP
    read_line (file1, line1, file1_eof);
    read_line (file2, line2, file2_eof);

    IF (file1_eof AND file2_eof)
    THEN
        retval := TRUE;
        EXIT;
    ELSIF (line1 != line2)
    THEN
        retval := FALSE;
        EXIT;
    ELSIF (file1_eof OR file2_eof)
    THEN
        retval := FALSE;
        EXIT;
    END IF;
END LOOP;
```

Then rewrite this loop body as follows:

```
LOOP
    read_line (file1, line1, file1_eof);
    read_line (file2, line2, file2_eof);

    IF (file1_eof AND file2_eof)
    THEN
        retval := TRUE;
        exit_loop := TRUE;
    ELSIF (line1 != line2)
    THEN
        retval := FALSE;
        exit_loop := TRUE;
    ELSIF (file1_eof OR file2_eof)
    THEN
        retval := FALSE;
        exit_loop := TRUE;
    END IF;
    EXIT WHEN exit_loop;
END LOOP;
```

Sometimes it can be difficult to come up with just one EXIT statement. This usually occurs when you need to check a condition at the beginning and end of a loop. If you run into this situation, consider changing to a WHILE loop.

You should also be careful to initialize your return value and your loop terminator variable, to avoid unwanted NULL values that might disrupt your logic.

### Benefits

A single EXIT is especially important in large, complex loop bodies; it allows you to more easily trace and debug your code.

### Challenges

Depending on how badly the loop was written initially, you may need to perform substantial restructuring to improve the loop code.

## CTL-06: Use a simple loop to avoid redundant code required by a WHILE loop.

Generally, you should use a simple loop if you always want the body of the loop to execute at least once. You use a WHILE loop if you want to check before executing the body the first time. Since the WHILE loop performs its check "up front," the variables in the boundary expression must be initialized. The code to initialize is often the same code needed to move to the next iteration in the WHILE loop. This redundancy creates a challenge in both debugging and maintaining the code: how do you remember to look at and update both?

If you find yourself writing and running the same code before the WHILE loop and at end of the WHILE loop body, consider switching to a simple loop.

### Example

I write a procedure to calculate overdue charges for books; the maximum fine to be charged is $10, and I will stop processing when there are no overdue books for a given date. Here is my first attempt at the procedure body:

```
DECLARE
    l_fine PLS_INTEGER := 0;
    l_date DATE := SYSDATE;
    l_overdue_count NUMBER;
BEGIN
    l_overdue_count :=
        overdue_pkg.countem (
            borrower_id => borrower_in,
            l_date);

    WHILE (l_overdue_count > 0 AND l_fine < 10)
    LOOP
        update_fine_info (l_date, l_one_day_fine);

        l_fine := l_fine + l_one_day_fine;
        l_date := l_date + 1;
        l_overdue_count :=
            overdue_pkg.countem (
```

```
                borrower_id => borrower_in,
                l_date);
        END LOOP;
```

As is readily apparent, I duplicate the assignments of values to l_overdue_count. I would be far better off rewriting this code as follows:

```
DECLARE
    l_fine PLS_INTEGER := 0;
    l_date DATE := SYSDATE;
    l_overdue_count NUMBER;
BEGIN
    LOOP
        EXIT WHEN
            (l_overdue_count <= 0 OR l_fine >= 10)

        update_fine_info (l_date, l_one_day_fine);

        l_fine := l_fine + l_one_day_fine;

        l_date := l_date + 1;

        l_overdue_count :=
            overdue_pkg.countem (
                borrower_id => borrower_in,
                l_date);
    END LOOP;
```

### Benefits

You avoid redundant code, always bad news in a program, since it increases maintenance costs and the chance of introducing bugs into your code.

### Challenges

If you have established a habit early on of writing WHILE loops, it can be hard to (a) notice the redundancy and (b) change your style.

## CTL-07: Never declare the FOR loop index.

PL/SQL offers two kinds of FOR loops: numeric and cursor. Both have this general format:

```
FOR loop index IN loop range
LOOP
    loop body
END LOOP;
```

The *loop index* is either an integer or a record; in either case, it's implicitly declared by the PL/SQL runtime engine. The scope of the loop index variable is restricted to the body of the loop (between the LOOP and END LOOP statements).

You should never declare a variable for the loop. If you do declare the loop index variable, you are actually declaring a completely separate (recordtype or numeric) variable that will (best case) never be used or (worst case) used outside the loop in a way that is confusing and likely to introduce errors.

*Example*

The developer who worked on the library management system before Jim (a PL/SQL novice) created this procedure to delete books from the collection by title:

```
CREATE OR REPLACE PROCEDURE remove_titles (
    title_in IN book.title%TYPE,
)
IS
    CURSOR book_cur
    IS
      SELECT isbn, author FROM book
       WHERE title LIKE title_in;
    book_rec book_cur%ROWTYPE;
BEGIN
    FOR book_rec IN book_cur
    LOOP
        te_book.rem (book_rec.isbn);
    END LOOP;
END;
```

It works just fine (no bugs reported), but Jim has been asked to modify the procedure to display the last book removed. So he adds this code after the FOR loop:

```
    END LOOP;
    pl (book_rec.isbn || ' - ' ||
        book_rec.author);
END;
```

The code compiles, but Jim spends the next two hours banging his head against the wall trying to figure out why the last book information keeps coming up NULL. He doesn't question the existing code, since it worked and was written by a high-priced consultant. It must be Jim's fault.

In fact, the original code was faulty. The declaration of book_rec was unnecessary and made Jim's error possible.

*Benefits*

By avoiding unnecessary code, you make it less likely for programmers to introduce errors into the code at some later point.

You need not take out "programmer's insurance": "Gee, I don't know if I need to declare that or not, so I'd better declare it." Instead, you make certain you understand how PL/SQL works and write appropriate code.

---

# CTL-08: Scan collections using FIRST, LAST, and NEXT in loops.

A collection in PL/SQL is like a single-dimensional array. A collection differs from an array, however, in that two of the three types of collections (nested tables and index-by tables) can be sparse, which means that the defined rows in the collection need not be sequentially defined. You can, in other words, assign a value to row 10 and a value to row 10,000, and now rows will exist between those two.

If you scan a collection with a FOR loop and the collection is sparse, the FOR loop tries to access an undefined row and raise a NO_DATA_FOUND exception. Instead, use the FIRST and NEXT methods to scan forward through a collection, and use LAST and PRIOR to scan backwards

## Example

I have decided to help all of my co-programmers by providing a package that offers a standard collection type (list of strings) and some utility programs to manipulate collections defined on that type. Here is the package specification:

```
CREATE OR REPLACE PACKAGE mycollection
IS
    TYPE string_tt IS TABLE OF VARCHAR2 (2000)
        INDEX BY BINARY_INTEGER;

    PROCEDURE show (list_in IN string_tt);

    FUNCTION eq (list1_in IN string_tt, list2_in IN string_tt)
        RETURN BOOLEAN;
END mycollection;
```

By using this package, I can easily declare a collection, display its contents, and even compare two collections of the same type to see if they are equal. That sounds handy! The implementation of this utility package, however, will determine how widely my code is used. Here's my first attempt:

```
CREATE OR REPLACE PACKAGE BODY mycollection
IS
    PROCEDURE show (list_in IN string_tt)
    IS
    BEGIN
        FOR indx IN list_in.FIRST .. list_in.LAST
        LOOP
            pl (list_in (indx));
        END LOOP;
    END show;

    FUNCTION eq (list1_in IN string_tt, list2_in IN string_tt)
        RETURN BOOLEAN
    IS
        retval      BOOLEAN     := TRUE;
        indx        PLS_INTEGER := list1_in.FIRST;
        l_last1     PLS_INTEGER := list1_in.LAST;
    BEGIN
        WHILE retval
            AND indx <= l_last1
        LOOP
            retval := list1_in (indx) = list2_in (indx);
            indx := indx + 1;
        END LOOP;
    RETURN retval;
    END eq;
END mycollection;
/
```

At first glance, this seems fine. I throw together a test and am pleased with the
results, as shown here:

```
SQL> DECLARE
  2      family   mycollection.string_tt;
  3      pets     mycollection.string_tt;
  4  BEGIN
  5      family (1) := 'Veva';
  6      family (2) := 'Eli';
  7      family (3) := 'Chris';
  8      family (4) := 'Steven';
  9      mycollection.show (family);
 10      pets (1) := 'Mercury';
 11      pets (2) := 'Moshe Jacobawitz';
 12      pets (3) := 'Sister Itsacat';
 13      bpl (mycollection.eq (family, pets));
 14  END;
 15  /
Veva
Eli
Chris
Steven
FALSE
```

Those two collections certainly aren't identical. Well, what a handy little package! I
enthusiastically tell all my programming friends that I have a present for them and
invite them to use mycollection. Not an hour goes by before Sriniva asks me to
visit her cubicle. "What's this all about?" she asks me (with a subtext of "Gee, I
guess your code is not to be trusted..."):

```
SQL> DECLARE
  2      authors   mycollection.string_tt;
  3      pets      mycollection.string_tt;
  4  BEGIN
  5      FOR rec IN (SELECT * FROM author)
  6      LOOP
  7          authors (rec.author_id) := rec.last_name;
  8      END LOOP;
  9
 10      mycollection.show (authors);
 11  END;
 12  /
FEUERSTEIN
DECLARE
*
ERROR at line 1:
ORA-01403: no data found
ORA-06512: at "SCOTT.MYCOLLECTION", line 8
```

I scratch my head for a while, then ask to see the data in the authors table. "Why
should that matter?" is the response. It's a good response. Embarrassment soon
propels me to the heart of the difficulty: her author_id values are probably not
sequential—but my loops assume a densely filled collection!

Check out the *myCollection.pkg* file for a rewrite of the package body that fixes
this problem.

### Benefits

Your scan is less likely to raise an exception.

This is the most efficient way to scan a collection. You can, as is shown in the files listed under "Resources," build protection within the FOR loop to avoid raising NO_DATA_FOUND, but then you might well do excessive looping. What if, for example, the second_row_in were two million?

### Resources

*plsqlloops.pro*: Script to compare the performance of several alternatives to scanning a collection.

*myCollection.pkg*: Implementation of a utility package that displays the contents of a collection and compares the contents of two collections.

## CTL-09: Move static expressions outside of loops and SQL statements.

Whenever you set out to tune your PL/SQL programs, you should first take a look at your loops. Any inefficiency inside a loop's body will be magnified by the multiple executions of that code.

A common mistake is to put code that is static or unchanging for each iteration of the loop inside the body. When you can identify such situations, extract the static code, assign the outcomes of that code to one or more variables, and then reference those variables inside the loop.

### Example

This procedure summarizes book reviews. It's run every morning at 8 A.M. and takes about 15 minutes to complete:

```
CREATE OR REPLACE PROCEDURE summarize_reviews (
    summary_title_in IN VARCHAR2,
    isbn_in IN book.isbn%TYPE)
IS
    CURSOR review_cur IS
        SELECT text,
                TO_CHAR (SYSDATE, 'MM/DD/YYYY') today
          FROM book_review
         WHERE isbn = isbn_in;
BEGIN
    FOR review_rec IN review_cur
    LOOP
        IF LENGTH (review_rec.text) > 100
        THEN
            review_rec.text :=
                SUBSTR (review_rec.text, 1, 100);
        END IF;

        review_pkg.summarize (
            UPPER (summary_title_in),
            today,
```

```
            UPPER (review_rec.text)
            );
     END LOOP;
END;
/
```

There are a number of problems with this code:

- Since my job starts and finishes on the same day, I don't need to select SYS-DATE with each row of my query. And unless I really want "today" to be a string expression, or I am ready to absorb the overhead of multiple implicit conversions, I should use TRUNC to get rid of the time element.

- I write over the text field of the review_rec record. While this is allowed by PL/SQL, you are generally better off not modifying the index variable loop. Treat it as a constant.

- Since my summary_title_in argument never changes, I shouldn't UPPER case in each iteration of the loop.

- Rather than check the length of the text for each row and then SUBSTR (and UPPER case), why not just SUBSTR inside SQL?

Here is a rewrite of the summarize_reviews procedure:

```
CREATE OR REPLACE PROCEDURE summarize_reviews (
     summary_title_in IN VARCHAR2,
     isbn_in IN book.isbn%TYPE)
IS
     l_summary book_types.summary_t
        := UPPER (summary_title_in);

     l_today CONSTANT DATE := TRUNC (SYSDATE);

     CURSOR review_cur IS
        SELECT UPPER (SUBSTR (text, 1, 100)) text
          FROM book_review
         WHERE isbn = isbn_in;
BEGIN
     FOR review_rec IN review_cur
     LOOP
        review_pkg.summarize (
           l_summary, l_today, review_rec.text
           );
     END LOOP;
END;
/
```

 You can, in general, expect the performance of built-in functions such as SUBSTR to work more efficiently in SQL than in PL/SQL, so move the processing to the SQL layer whenever possible.

## Benefits

Your code doesn't do any unnecessary work and so executes more efficiently.

### Challenges

Don't be obsessed with this sort of optimization as you write your code. It's theo-retically true that calling UPPER just once before the loop is more efficient compared to calling it 100 times inside the loop. It's also very likely to be the case that the cycles saved on this optimization are never noticed by the user. You are always better off saving the bulk of your optimization efforts until you have identi-fied the bottlenecks in your application as a whole.

### Resources

*insql.sql*: A script to compare the performance of functions in SQL versus PL/SQL.

# Miscellaneous

The best practices in this section are grouped together simply because they don't fall into either of the other categories.

## CTL-10: Use anonymous blocks within IF statements to conserve resources.

One of the nice things about PL/SQL is that you, the developer, can define any set of executable statements as a distinct block, with its own declaration, executable, and exception sections.

If you notice that certain operations and data structures aren't needed unless a certain condition is satisfied, move all the execution of those operations and the declaration of those data structures inside the conditional statement. The result is that you won't incur the overhead (CPU or memory) unless it's absolutely needed.

### Example

In the following block, I declare a set of local variables and even initialize l_name with a function that usually takes 10 seconds to execute (min_balance_account). But when I write my block, it turns out that in many situations, those structures are ignored:

```
DECLARE
    TYPE account_tabtype IS TABLE
        OF account%ROWTYPE INDEX BY BINARY_INTEGER;
    l_accounts account_tabtype;

    l_name VARCHAR2(2000) :=
        min_balance_account (SYSDATE);
BEGIN
    IF balance_too_low (1056)
    THEN
        use_collection (l_accounts);
        use_name (l_name);
    ELSE
```

```
                -- No use of l_accounts or l_name
                ...
        END IF;
    END;
```

Once I recognize this situation (usually identified through a code walkthrough), I should change it to this:

```
BEGIN
    IF balance_too_low (1056)
    THEN
        DECLARE
            TYPE account_tabtype IS TABLE
                OF account%ROWTYPE
                INDEX BY BINARY_INTEGER;
            l_accounts account_tabtype;

            l_name VARCHAR2(2000) :=
                min_balance_account (SYSDATE);
        BEGIN
            use_collection (l_accounts);
            use_name (l_name);
        END;
    ELSE
        -- No use of l_accounts or l_name
        ...
    END IF;
END;
```

### Benefits

Your programs won't execute unnecessary code, improving performance and reducing memory requirements for the program.

### Challenges

It can be hard to realize as you first write your program that this kind of situation exists. Use code walkthroughs to uncover these optimization opportunities. You can also use Oracle8*i*'s code profiler (the DBMS_PROFILER built-in package) to identify unused or little-used code. A number of PL/SQL IDEs offer a GUI interface to this profiler.

### Resources

The following products currently offer GUIs to DBMS_PROFILER:

*http://www.quest.com/sql_navigator/*: SQL Navigator.

*http://www.sfi-software.com/sql-programmer.htm*: SQL Programmer.

*http://www.embarcadero.com/products/Develop/develop.htm*: Rapid SQL.

## CTL-11: Label and highlight GOTOs if using this normally unnecessary construct.

I suppose that it was thorough of Oracle to include a GOTO statement in the PL/SQL language. This statement, however, should generally be avoided, as it leads to unstructured code design that is hard to analyze and debug.

There are scenarios in which a GOTO can be justified; these mostly relate to going into existing spaghetti code to fix a bug or enhance the code. For an extensive review of GOTO-related issues, see Chapter 16 in Steve McConnell's book, *Code Complete.*

### Example

Here is a use of GOTO that calls attention to itself:

```
CREATE OR REPLACE PROCEDURE someone_elses_mess
/*
|| Author: Longgone Consultant
|| Maintained by: Sad Employee
||
|| Modification History
|| When    Who     What
|| --------------------------------------------
|| 11/2000 Sad E. Fixed bug in overdue logic.
||                Used GOTO to bypass Gordian
||                Knot of code left by L.C.
*/
IS
BEGIN
   IF ... THEN
      IF ... THEN
         FOR rec IN cur LOOP
            -- 11/2000 Bypass with GOTO
            GOTO <<quick_exit>>
         END LOOP;
         ... lots more code
      END IF;
      -- 11/2000 GOTO Target
      <<quick_exit>>
   END IF;
```

### Benefits

Even if you can, at times, justify the use of a GOTO, you can almost always achieve the same effect with a more structured and more easily understood use of conditional and loop logic.

### Resources

*Code Complete,* by Steve McConnell: See Chapter 16, *Unusual Control Structures,* for an in-depth discussion of the GOTO statement and recommendations for when it can justifiably be used.

# 5

# *Exception*
# *Handling*

Even if you write such amazing code that it contains no errors and never acts inappropriately, your users might still *use* your program incorrectly. The result? Situations that cause programs to fail. PL/SQL provides *exceptions*, a flexible and powerful architecture that raises, traps, and handles errors.

Before getting into specific best practices, you should be sure to understand how exception handling works. For example, remember that an exception section handles only errors raised in the executable section of the block, not errors raised in the declaration section.

Next and even more important, I offer the following meta-best practice of this chapter.

## *EXC-00: Set guidelines for application-wide error handling before you start coding.*

It's impractical to define EXCEPTION sections in your code after the fact—in other words, after the programs have been written. The best way to implement application-wide, consistent error handling is to use a standardized package that contains at least the following elements:

- Procedures that perform most exception-handling tasks, such as writing to an error log.
- A raise program that hides the complexity of RAISE_APPLICATION_ERROR and application-specific error numbers.
- A function that returns error message text for a given error number.

These ideas are covered in specific best practices in this chapter. A simple error-handling package may be found in the *err.pkg* file on the Oracle PL/SQL Best Practices web site.

# Raising Exceptions

The following best practices cover how to check for conditions that might require the raising of an exception, deciding how to propagate exception information, and how to best raise exceptions.

## EXC-01: Verify preconditions using standardized assertion routines that raise violation exceptions.

Every time you write a program, you make certain assumptions. A user of your program doesn't necessarily know about those assumptions. If you don't "code defensively" and make sure that your assumptions aren't violated, your programs can break down in unpredictable ways.

Use assertion routines to make it as easy as possible to validate assumptions in a declarative fashion. These routines, standardized for an entire application, take care of all the housekeeping: what to do when a condition fails, how to report the problem, and whether and how to stop the program from continuing.

### Example

Here's a simple assertion program that checks to see if a condition is TRUE. If the condition is FALSE or NULL, the procedure displays a message to the screen and then raises an exception (if so desired) with dynamic PL/SQL (this implementation relies on Oracle8*i*'s native dynamic SQL):

```
CREATE OR REPLACE PROCEDURE assert (
    condition_in IN BOOLEAN,
    message_in IN VARCHAR2,
    raise_exception_in IN BOOLEAN := TRUE,
    exception_in IN VARCHAR2
        := 'VALUE_ERROR'
)
IS
BEGIN
    IF    NOT condition_in
       OR condition_in IS NULL
    THEN
        pl ('Assertion Failure!');
        pl (message_in);

        IF raise_exception_in
        THEN
            EXECUTE IMMEDIATE
                'BEGIN RAISE ' || exception_in || '; END;';
        END IF;
    END IF;
END assert;
```

With this program in place, you can easily, and in a declarative fashion, make sure that all inputs are hunky-dory before proceeding with your business logic. Here's an example:

```
BEGIN
    assert (isbn_in IS NOT NULL,
      'The ISBN must be provided.');

    assert (page_count_in < 2000,
      'Readers don't like big, fat books!');
```

### Benefits

With easy-to-use, declarative assertion routines, you're more likely to actually check for valid inputs and conditions.

Validation will occur in a standard way throughout your application if everyone uses the same assertion programs.

### Challenges

Develop a habit of thinking through and asserting all your assumptions at the top of your executable section, before you start writing any business logic.

### Resources

*assert.pro*: A simple assertion procedure

*assert.pkg*: An assertion package that offers assertions for different conditions

---

## EXC-02: Use the default exception-handling model to communicate module status back to calling PL/SQL programs.

Watch out for carrying baggage from other languages into the world of PL/SQL. Your last language might not have had a sophisticated error-handling architecture. As a consequence, you relied on parameters in every program to pass back error status (code and message).

Don't do this in PL/SQL! Rely on the default model: raise exceptions and handle those exceptions in the separate exception section of your blocks.

### Example

Here's the kind of code you want to avoid:

```
BEGIN
    overdue.analyze_status (
        title_in,
        start_date_in,
        error_code,
        error_msg);

    IF error_code != 0
    THEN
        err.log (...);
```

```
          GOTO end_of_program;
    END IF;

    overdue.send_report (
        error_code,
        error_msg);

    IF error_code != 0
    THEN
        err.log (...);
        GOTO end_of_program;
    END IF;
```

### Benefits

Your executable sections are clean, simple, and easy to follow. You don't have to check for status after every program call. You simply include an exception section to trap and deal with crises as they arise.

### Challenges

It can be hard to break old habits.

You might inherit code that looks like the example. In this case, I would suggest to your manager that it's worth it to proactively clean up the code.

If you are calling PL/SQL from a non-Oracle frontend, you may *need* to pass back error information (see **EXC-03**).

---

## EXC-03: Catch all exceptions and convert to meaningful return codes before returning to non-PL/SQL host programs.

Suppose that you are calling PL/SQL programs from Visual Basic, Powerbuilder, Java, or some other language. These non-Oracle development languages may not understand, or be able to handle, PL/SQL exceptions very gracefully. In this situation, you may need to pass back error status (code and message) with at least some of your programs.

You should do this only on an "exception" basis—as needed. The best way to do it is to overload the original program in your package with another of the same name and two additional parameters.

### Example

Suppose you need to call overdue.analyze_status both from within the Oracle RDBMS (i.e., from another stored procedure) and from within a Visual Basic application. You can use package overloading to offer the "same" program with a different interface:

```
CREATE OR REPLACE PACKAGE overdue
IS
    PROCEDURE analyze_status (
        title_in IN book.title%TYPE,
        start_date_in IN DATE := SYSDATE);
```

```
overdue.analyze_status (
   title_in IN book.title%TYPE,
   start_date_in IN DATE := SYSDATE,
   error_code OUT INTEGER,
   error_msg OUT VARCHAR2);
```

### Benefits

Developers can call PL/SQL stored code and gracefully check for errors in the way that's most appropriate in their own programming language.

The datatype for the error code and message must be generic ANSI SQL types, not Oracle-specific types. For example, you can't use a BOOLEAN parameter or PL/SQL index-by table as a return value for any function that interfaces with non-PL/SQL tools.

## EXC-04: Use your own raise procedure in place of explicit calls to RAISE_APPLICATION_ERROR.

When it comes to managing errors, Oracle requires a lot of developers. If you're raising a "system" exception like NO_DATA_FOUND, you use RAISE. But when you want to raise an application-specific error, you use RAISE_APPLICATION_ ERROR. If you use the latter, you have to provide an error number and message. This leads to unnecessary and damaging hard coding (see **EXC-09**).

A more fail-safe approach is to provide a predefined raise procedure that automatically checks the error number and determines the correct way to raise the error. An example of such a procedure may be found in the *err.pkg* file on the Oracle PL/SQL Best Practices web site, and is described briefly in the following section.

### Example

Instead of writing code like this:

```
RAISE_APPLICATION_ERROR (
   -20734,
   'Employee must be 18 years old.');
```

you should write code like this:

```
err.raise (errnums.emp_too_young);
```

Here's an example of how you might construct a generic exception raiser (from *err.pkg*):

```
PROCEDURE raise (
   errcode   IN    PLS_INTEGER := NULL,
   errmsg    IN    VARCHAR2 := NULL
)
IS
   l_errcode   PLS_INTEGER := NVL (errcode, SQLCODE);
   l_errmsg    PLS_INTEGER := NVL (errmsg, SQLERRM);
BEGIN
   IF l_errcode BETWEEN -20999 AND -20000
```

```
       THEN
          RAISE_APPLICATION_ERROR (l_errcode, l_errmsg);

       /* Use positive error numbers -- lots to choose from! */
       ELSIF     l_errcode > 0
             AND l_errcode NOT IN (1, 100)
       THEN
          RAISE_APPLICATION_ERROR (-20000, l_errcode || '-' || l_errmsg);

       /* Re-raise any other exception using dynamic PL/SQL. */
       ELSIF l_errcode != 0
       THEN
          PLVdyn.plsql (
          'DECLARE myexc EXCEPTION; ' ||
          '   PRAGMA EXCEPTION_INIT (myexc, '
               || TO_CHAR (l_errcode) || ');'
        ||'BEGIN  RAISE myexc; END;'
            );
       END IF;
    END;
```

### Benefits

Individual developers don't have to make judgment calls about how they should raise the exception (RAISE? RAISE_APPLICATION_ERROR?). They simply pass the appropriate error number (hopefully identified via a named constant) and let the raise "engine" do the heavy lifting.

You can choose to use positive error numbers for your own application-specific exceptions. By taking this approach, you aren't constrained to error numbers between –20,999 and –20,000, some of which Oracle also uses. The **err.raise** procedure intercepts positive error numbers and passes them back to the calling program as an exception by bundling the error number and message into a single string in the call to RAISE_APPLICATION_ERROR.

### Challenges

First, you must set your standards on what kind of exceptions (the numbers and messages, in particular) you will use for your application. Then you need to make sure that everyone uses the err.raise procedure.

### Resources

*err.pkg*: A simple, but functional prototype of a generic error-handling package.

---

## EXC-05: Only RAISE exceptions for errors, not to branch execution control.

The RAISE statement is an easy and powerful way to abort normal processing in a program and immediately "go to" the appropriate WHEN handler. You should, however, never use RAISE in this way. You should raise an exception only when an error has occurred, not to control program flow.

## Example

Here's a program that demonstrates the problem; it performs a full table scan of a collection and immediately exits when it finds a match. The exit_function exception aborts the function if the input title is NULL; it's also used as the last line in the function:

```
CREATE OR REPLACE FUNCTION book_from_list (
    list_in IN book_tabtype,
    title_in IN book.title%TYPE)
RETURN book%ROWTYPE
IS
    exit_function EXCEPTION;
BEGIN
    IF title_in IS NULL
    THEN
        RAISE exit_function;
    END IF;

    FOR indx IN list_in.FIRST .. list_in.LAST
    LOOP
        IF list_in(indx).title = title_in
        THEN
            RETURN list_in(indx);
        END IF;
    END LOOP;

    RAISE exit_function;

EXCEPTION
    WHEN exit_function THEN RETURN NULL;
END;
```

Whew. Strange stuff. You manage to make it all the way to the end of the function, and then you are punished by having an exception raised! This is very poorly structured code: hard to understand and hard to maintain.

Here's a better approach:

```
CREATE OR REPLACE FUNCTION book_from_list (
    list_in IN book_tabtype,
    title_in IN book.title%TYPE)
RETURN book%ROWTYPE
IS
    indx PLS_INTEGER;
    retval book%ROWTYPE;
BEGIN
    IF title_in IS NOT NULL
    THEN
        indx := list_in.FIRST;
        LOOP
            IF list_in(indx).title = title_in
            THEN
                retval := list_in(indx);
            END IF;
```

```
        indx := list_in.NEXT (indx);
     END LOOP;
  END IF;
  RETURN retval;
END;
```

Be on the lookout for a clear symptom of this misuse of error handling: declared exceptions whose names describe actions (exit_function) rather than errors (null_title).

### Benefits

Your code is more straightforward and is easier to read, debug, and maintain.

## EXC-06: Do not overload an exception with multiple errors unless the loss of information is intentional.

Don't declare one generic exception such as bad_data and then raise that exception under different circumstances. Users of your code will have trouble understanding precisely what caused the problem. Instead, declare a separate exception for each different kind of failure.

### Example

Oracle is guilty of violating this best practice, as can be seen with NO_DATA_ FOUND. This exception can be raised by a SELECT INTO that finds no rows, by attempting to read an undefined row in a collection, or by reading past the end of a file. How can you tell what went wrong inside your NO_DATA_FOUND handler? This dilemma is shown in this example:

```
CREATE OR REPLACE PROCEDURE two_reads
IS
   l_title book.title%TYPE;
   l_line VARCHAR2(1023);
   fid UTL_FILE.FILE_TYPE;
BEGIN
   SELECT title INTO l_title
     FROM emp
    WHERE 1 = 2;

   fid := UTL_FILE.FOPEN (
      'c:\temp', 'justoneline.txt', 'R');
   UTL_FILE.GET_LINE (fid, l_line);
   UTL_FILE.GET_LINE (fid, l_line);

EXCEPTION
   WHEN NO_DATA_FOUND
   THEN
      pl ('Who did that?');
END two_reads;
```

If you do run into situations like this, whether due to Oracle's design or another developer in your organization, you can use nested blocks to avoid the ambiguity. By declaring a block around a set of lines of code, you can restrict the propagation of the ambiguous exception and transform that exception into a unique identifier. Here's an example of this approach:

```
CREATE OR REPLACE PROCEDURE two_reads
IS
    l_title book.title%TYPE;
    l_line VARCHAR2(1023);
    fid UTL_FILE.FILE_TYPE;
    no_table_data EXCEPTION;
    no_file_data EXCEPTION;
BEGIN
    BEGIN
        SELECT title INTO l_title
          FROM emp
         WHERE 1 = 2;
    EXCEPTION
        WHEN NO_DATA_FOUND THEN RAISE no_table_data;
    END;

    BEGIN
        fid := UTL_FILE.FOPEN ('c:\temp', 'justoneline.txt', 'R');
        UTL_FILE.GET_LINE (fid, l_line);
        UTL_FILE.GET_LINE (fid, l_line);
    EXCEPTION
        WHEN NO_DATA_FOUND THEN RAISE no_file_data;
    END;

EXCEPTION
    WHEN no_table_data
    THEN
        pl ('Query on table returned no data!');
    WHEN no_file_data
    THEN
        pl ('Attempt to read past end-of-file!');
END two_reads;
```

### Benefits

Developers can check for, and handle, the different kinds of errors your code might produce.

### Resources

*excquiz6.sql* and *excquiz6a.sql*: Demonstrations of how you can transform a single, overused exception such as NO_DATA_FOUND into multiple, distinct exceptions.

# Handling Exceptions

Once an exception is raised, it generally needs to be handled. These best practices offer advice on writing exception-handling sections.

## EXC-07: Handle exceptions that cannot be avoided but can be anticipated.

If you are writing a program in which you can predict that a certain error will occur, you should include a handler in your code for that, allowing for a graceful and informative failure.

The form that this failure takes doesn't, by the way, necessarily need to be an exception. When writing functions, you may well decide that in the case of certain exceptions, you will want to return a value such as NULL, rather than allow an exception to propagate out of the function.

### Example

This recommendation is easily demonstrated with the ubiquitous SELECT INTO lookup query. An error that often occurs is NO_DATA_FOUND, which indicates that the query didn't identify any rows. Now, following SQL-04, I put SELECT INTO inside a function, but I don't allow the NO_DATA_FOUND exception to propagate out of the function:

```
CREATE OR REPLACE FUNCTION book_title (
    isbn_in IN book.isbn%TYPE)
RETURN book.title%TYPE
IS
    l_ title book.title%TYPE;
BEGIN
    SELECT title INTO l_title
      FROM book
     WHERE isbn =isbn_in;
    RETURN l_rec.title;
EXCEPTION
    WHEN NO_DATA_FOUND
    THEN
        RETURN NULL;
END;
```

In other words, if the ISBN passed to the function finds no book, return NULL for the title. This is an unambiguous indicator of failure; a book *must* have a title.

I have decided in this case not to allow NO_DATA_FOUND to propagate (go unhandled) out of the function. I use a SELECT INTO (implicit query) to fetch the book title; Oracle's implementation of implicit queries means that NO_DATA_ FOUND (as well as TOO_MANY_ROWS) might be raised. That doesn't mean, however, that within my function, it really *is* an exception when no row is found. In fact, I might be expecting to not find a match.

By returning NULL rather than propagating an exception, I leave it up to the user of my function to decide how to deal with a "no row found" situation. She might raise an exception, as in:

```
BEGIN
    l_title := book_title (l_isbn);
    IF l_title IS NULL
```

```
THEN
    RAISE NO_DATA_FOUND;
END IF;
```

or she might decide that such a result means that everything is, in fact, as desired:

```
BEGIN
    l_title := book_title (l_isbn);
    IF l_title IS NULL
    THEN
        process_new_book (l_isbn);
    END IF;
```

### Benefits

Your programs are better-behaved and more likely to be useful and used. If you let the exception propagate out, this function would be unpredictable and hard to integrate into your application, since exception handlers must be coded in the caller's code block.

### Challenges

It's one thing to set a standard, and quite another to have everyone implement programs according to the standard. See **MOD-02** for ideas on generating functions that comply with your best practices.

---

## EXC-08: Avoid hard-coded exposure of error handling by using standard, declarative procedures.

The best way to achieve consistent, high-quality error handling throughout your application is to offer a set of predefined procedures that do the basic plumbing of error handling: record the error information if desired, propagate the exception, and so on.

It's crucial then to make certain that development team members always and only use these procedures in their WHEN clauses.

### Example

Here's the kind of code you should never write inside an exception handler:

```
EXCEPTION
    WHEN NO_DATA_FOUND THEN
        v_msg := 'No company for id ' || TO_CHAR (v_id);
        v_err := SQLCODE;
        v_prog := 'fixdebt';
        INSERT INTO errlog VALUES
            (v_err, v_msg, v_prog, SYSDATE, USER);


    WHEN OTHERS THEN
        v_err := SQLCODE;
        v_msg := SQLERRM;
        v_prog := 'fixdebt';
```

```
            INSERT INTO errlog VALUES
                (v_err, v_msg, v_prog, SYSDATE, USER);
            RAISE;
```

There are several problems with this code:

- Exposure of logging method. What if you change the structure of the table, or decide to write to a file instead? Every handler has to change.

- Hard-coded program names. This information is available from the built-in function DBMS_UTILITY.FORMAT_CALL STACK.

A better approach is to rely on predefined handlers. Here's a rewrite of the same exception section:

```
EXCEPTION
    WHEN NO_DATA_FOUND THEN
        err.handle (
            'No company for id ' || TO_CHAR (v_id),
            log => TRUE,
            reraise => FALSE);
    WHEN OTHERS THEN
        err.handle (log => TRUE, reraise => TRUE);
```

### Benefits

All developers handle errors in the same way, achieving consistency in logging and also in user presentation of error feedback.

Enhancements or changes in logging standards can be easily (almost instantly) implemented.

### Challenges

Well, you need to implement the generic package, but the predefined procedure gives you a functional starting point for that.

Developers must be trained in using the package, and then they must use it.

Use code walkthroughs and/or automated code analysis to ensure that programmers are following the standard.

### Resources

*err.pkg*: A simple, but functional prototype of a generic error-handling package.

---

## EXC-09: Use named constants to soft-code application-specific error numbers and messages.

Oracle allocates 1000 error numbers, between –20,000 and –20,999, to use for our own application-specific errors (such as "Employee must be 18 years old" or "Reservation date must be in the future").

Define all error numbers and their associated messages in a database table or operating-system file. Build a package that gives names to these errors, and then raise the errors using those names and not any hard-coded values.

## Example

Here's a fairly typical tangle of hard-coded, error-prone programming with RAISE_ APPLICATION_ERROR. Sam Developer is told to write a procedure to stop updates and inserts when an employee is younger than 18. Sam thinks to himself "Surely no one has used error 20734 yet, so I will use it" and produces this code:

```
CREATE OR REPLACE PROCEDURE check_hiredate (
    date_in IN DATE)
IS
BEGIN
    IF date_in < ADD_MONTHS (SYSDATE, -1 * 12 * 18)
    THEN
        RAISE_APPLICATION_ERROR (
            -20734,
            'Employee must be 18 years old.');
    END IF;
END;
```

Check out all that hard-coding! And while Sam is writing his code, of course, Natasha Programmer also decides that 20734 is a fine error number. What a mess! Here's a much cleaner approach:

```
CREATE OR REPLACE PROCEDURE check_hiredate (
    date_in IN DATE)
IS
BEGIN
    IF emp_rules.emp_too_young (date_in)
    THEN
        err.raise (errnums.emp_too_young);
    END IF;
END;
```

First, I have moved the logic defining a "too young" employee to a function, as recommended in **MOD-01**. For error handling, Sam now simply knows that he calls the err.raise procedure to raise his error. Which error? Sam goes to the list of predefined exceptions (either in documentation or via a GUI interface) and picks, by name, the one that matches.

## Benefits

Developers avoid conflicts over the same error number; such conflicts can lead to massive confusion.

Developers don't have to decide the best way to raise an error. Just call the err.raise procedure and let it do the work for you.

## Challenges

The same as for **EXC-08** (predefined handler procedures).

You need to build code and data to maintain known errors, associated with numbers and error text.

### Resources

*msginfo.pkg*: Infrastructure package and associated table to manage error numbers and text, and to generate a package with named exceptions.

## EXC-10: Include standardized modules in packages to dump package state when errors occur.

When an error occurs in one of your PL/SQL blocks, it's often useful to determine the values of persistent package variables at the time of the failure. You can do this to some extent with the debuggers available with many IDEs. That approach doesn't, however, give you access to the data values within a user's application session.

One way to obtain this information is to write a "dump" procedure in each of your packages. This dump procedure displays or records the contents of any relevant variables or data structures—whatever you determine is of value inside that package. You can then feed this information to an error handler, to provide as much information as possible to the person debugging your code.

Providing such dump procedures can dramatically reduce the time spent inserting debug messages only to be removed later, as well as to record problems that appear intermittently, and are hard to reproduce.

This approach obviously relies on the conformance to standards established in advance, so that method names and stack formats can be interpreted, but all of these details can be hidden from view in a package, such as the *error_pkg* included in the *callstack.sql* file (see the "Resources" section).

This package (provided by Dwayne King, ace reviewer and PL/SQL developer) keeps track of the call stack by recording in a PL/SQL table each piece of code as it "announces" itself. It then uses that stack to determine which dump methods need to be called when an error occurs.

Unfortunately, there's no reliable (and supported) way right now to easily determine which packages "have state" even if they aren't in the call stack, but this may be possible in the future. Another straightforward exercise is to extend this package to write to a log file or pipe instead of just using the standard DBMS_OUTPUT package.

### Example

The *demo_pkg* file (see the "Resources" section) conforms to the "dump API" by including a procedure named instantiate_error_context in the specification:

```
CREATE OR REPLACE PACKAGE demo_pkg
IS
    PROCEDURE proc1;

    PROCEDURE instantiate_error_context;
END;
/
```

The proc1 procedure sets the module name in the stack, assigns a value to a variable, and then calls proc2, which also "announces" itself and modifies a package variable. It then, however, raises an EXCEPTION:

```
PROCEDURE demo_pkg.proc1 IS
BEGIN
    --announce entry into this module
    error_pkg.set_module_name ('demo_pkg.proc1');

    -- Application processing here.
    application.field_1 := 'test string';

    proc2;

    error_pkg.remove_module_name;
EXCEPTION
    WHEN OTHERS
    THEN
        error_pkg.set_err_msg ('DAT023');
        error_pkg.raise_error ('Failed Operation');
END;
```

The instantiation procedure passes the values of the package data (the package state) to the error package:

```
PROCEDURE demo_pkg.instantiate_error_context
IS
BEGIN
    error_pkg.add_context (
        'DEMO_PKG', 'Field #1', application.field_1);
    error_pkg.add_context (
        'DEMO_PKG', 'Field #2', application.field_2);
    error_pkg.add_context (
        'DEMO_PKG', 'Field #3', application.field_3);
END;
```

When you run demo_pkg.proc1, you see the following output:

```
SQL> exec demo_pkg.proc1
Adding demo_pkg.proc1 to stack
Adding demo_pkg.proc2 to stack
Error Log Time:            13:15:33
Call Stack:                demo_pkg.proc1 --> demo_pkg.proc2
Comments:                  Failed Operation
CFRS Error No:             DAT027
Oracle Error:              ORA-01403: no data found
----------DEMO_PKG--------------------
Field #1:                  test string
Field #2:                  -37
Field #3:                  NULL
```

The *error_pkg* used in the example and found in the *callstack.sql* file requires you to explicitly list the packages that contain instantiate_error_context procedures. An improved implementation is to rely on dynamic SQL (either DBMS_SQL or native dynamic SQL) to automatically construct the program call and execute it.

### Benefits

Changes to the way errors are handled or logged don't require changing any code, other than the one generic raise procedure

You can validate that packages conform to the standard by querying ALL_ARGU-MENTS to check for packages that don't contain the instantiate_error_context procedure.

### Challenges

To be useful, a method like this relies on developers following previously defined standards.

### Resources

*callstack.sql*: Contains the error package and a demonstration package containing a dump procedure.

## EXC-11: Use WHEN OTHERS only for unknown exceptions that need to be trapped.

Don't use WHEN OTHERS to grab any and every error. If you know that a certain exception might be raised, include a handler for that specifically.

### Example

Here's an exception section that clearly expects a DUP_VAL_ON_INDEX error to be raised but that buries that information in WHEN OTHERS:

```
EXCEPTION
   WHEN OTHERS
   THEN
      IF SQLCODE = -1
      THEN
         update_instead (...);
      ELSE
         err.log;
         RAISE;
      END IF;
```

Here's a much better approach:

```
EXCEPTION
   WHEN DUP_VAL_ON_INDEX
   THEN
      update_instead (...);
```

```
WHEN OTHERS
THEN
    err.log;
    RAISE;
```

## Benefits

Your code more clearly states what you expect to have happen and how you want to handle your errors. That makes the code easier to maintain and enhance.

You avoid hard-coding error numbers in your checks against SQLCODE.

# Declaring Exceptions

In addition to raising and handling exceptions, you also must pay attention to how and when to declare exceptions and to assign names to error numbers.

---

### EXC-12: Standardize named application exceptions in package specifications.

It's likely that a developer will raise a certain error or errors in the process of using your code, you should declare exceptions in the package specification. Users of your code can then trap and handle those errors by name.

This approach is used most often for application-specific exceptions, but if your program might also raise an Oracle exception that has not been given a name in the STANDARD or other built-in package, you can give it a name and associate it with that number. See **EXC-14** for more details.

### Example

Suppose that my overdue.analyze_status procedure might raise one of the following two errors:

*"Overdue more than one month"*
    I have defined this as a serious error in my database. I must immediately stop processing and raise an exception.

*"Fetch out of sequence"*
    This is an Oracle error that occurs when something goes wrong in my cursor FOR loop.

I then add these lines to my overdue package:

```
CREATE OR REPLACE PACKAGE overdue
IS
    excessive_lateness EXCEPTION;
    PRAGMA EXCEPTION_INIT (
        excessive_lateness, -20700);

    fetch_out_of_sequence EXCEPTION;
    PRAGMA EXCEPTION_INIT (
        fetch_out_of_sequence, -1003);
```

### Benefits

Programmers have a better sense of what to expect—and what kind of exception handlers to write—when using your code.

### Resources

*sqlerr.pks*: Package of predefined exceptions that commonly occur when working with SQL, and especially dynamic SQL, inside PL/SQL.

## EXC-13: Document all package exceptions by module in package specifications.

Different programs may well raise different exceptions. You need to communicate this information clearly to users of your code so they know what to expect and what to code for. PL/SQL doesn't offer a structured way to do this as part of the language (Java, for example, does precisely that). So you need to come up with a standard convention for including such documentation in your code.

### Example

The following package specification offers one simple example of how you might document the exceptions individual programs might raise:

```
CREATE OR REPLACE PACKAGE overdue
IS
    PROCEDURE analyze_status (...);
        /* analyze_status can raise:
            overdue.excessive_lateness
            overdue.fetch_out_of_sequence
        */

    FUNCTION count_by_borrower (...)
        RETURN INTEGER;
        /* count_by_borrower can raise:
            NO_DATA_FOUND
            borrower.does_not_exist
        */
```

### Benefits

Programmers have a better sense of what to expect—and what kind of exception handlers to write—when using your code.

### Challenges

It can be hard to take the necessary time to do this. Define it as part of your standard documentation for packages; then use code walkthroughs to identify omissions.

## EXC-14: Use the EXCEPTION_INIT pragma to name system exceptions that might be raised by your program.

There are hundreds upon hundreds of Oracle error codes and messages. Only a small handful are actually assigned a name for use in the PL/SQL language. This assignment occurs in the STANDARD package; here, for example, is the code defining the first three named exceptions in that package:

```
CURSOR_ALREADY_OPEN exception;
   pragma EXCEPTION_INIT(CURSOR_ALREADY_OPEN, '-6511');

DUP_VAL_ON_INDEX exception;
   pragma EXCEPTION_INIT(DUP_VAL_ON_INDEX, '-0001');

TIMEOUT_ON_RESOURCE exception;
   pragma EXCEPTION_INIT(TIMEOUT_ON_RESOURCE, '-0051');
```

And since STANDARD is the default package, you can then write code in your own programs like:

```
EXCEPTION
   WHEN CURSOR_ALREADY_OPEN THEN ...
```

You can also give names to system exceptions, and you should do so when your program might raise one of those exceptions.

### Example

When I built PLVdyn, a PL/Vision package that makes it easier to execute dynamic SQL, I gave names to a number of errors that commonly occur when constructing and executing SQL strings with DBMS_SQL. I realized that no matter how good my code was, a user might pass a dynamic string that, for example, referenced an undefined table or column. Without a named exception, you ended up writing code like this:

```
BEGIN
   cur := PLVdyn.open_and_parse ('SELECT ... ');
   ...
EXCEPTION .
   WHEN OTHERS
   THEN
      IF SQLCODE = -904 THEN -- invalid column name
         ...
      ELSIF SQLCODE = -942 THEN - no such table
```

and so on. So I added a sequence of EXCEPTION_INIT pragmas, some of which are shown here:

```
CREATE OR REPLACE PACKAGE PLVdyn
IS
   /* Exceptions */
   no_such_table EXCEPTION;
      PRAGMA EXCEPTION_INIT (no_such_table, -942);
   invalid_table_name EXCEPTION;
      PRAGMA EXCEPTION_INIT (invalid_table_name, -903);
   invalid_column_name EXCEPTION;
      PRAGMA EXCEPTION_INIT (invalid_column_name, -904);
```

Now PL/Vision developers can write code like this:

```
BEGIN
   cur := PLVdyn.open_and_parse ('SELECT ... ');
   ...
EXCEPTION
   WHEN PLVdyn.invalid_column_name THEN
      ...
   WHEN PLVdyn.no_such_table THEN
```

## Benefits

You can trap exceptions by name instead of using conditional logic inside the WHEN OTHERS clause. The result is code that is much easier to read and also to maintain, since the logic for handling each exception is clearly segregated into different handlers.

## Challenges

None. In fact, you can always add these EXCEPTION_INIT pragmas after the fact (after, that is, you have written your package) and then retrofit existing exception sections to use the newly named exceptions.

## Resources

*sqlerr.pks*: Package of predefined exceptions that commonly occur when working with SQL, and especially dynamic SQL, inside PL/SQL.

# 6

## Writing SQL in PL/SQL

One of the reasons developers like PL/SQL so much is that it's so easy to write SQL inside a PL/SQL block of code.

One of the most dangerous aspects of PL/SQL is that it's so easy to write SQL inside a PL/SQL block of code.

Paradox? Irony? SQL is, in fact, a sort of Achilles heel of PL/SQL development. Now, given that PL/SQL was first conceived as a procedural language extension to SQL, such a statement should raise eyebrows even further. The simple fact of the matter, however, is that if you aren't careful about how you place SQL statements in your PL/SQL code, you will end up with applications that are difficult to optimize, debug, and manage over time.

You should follow several simple (to state) guidelines when working with SQL inside PL/SQL. I collect all of these together in the following meta-best practice of this chapter.

### SQL-00: Establish and follow clear rules for how to write SQL in your application.

- Never repeat a SQL statement.
- Encapsulate all SQL statements behind a procedural interface (usually a package).
- Write your code assuming that the underlying data structures will change.
- Take advantage of PL/SQL-specific enhancements for SQL.

All these topics—with examples, benefits, and challenges—are explored in the more detailed best practices in this chapter.

# General SQL and Transaction Management

This section contains some general-purpose best practices for writing SQL statements and some specific best practices for handling transactions.

## SQL-01: Qualify PL/SQL variables with their scope names when referenced inside SQL statements.

You *could* declare a variable that has the same name as a table, a column, or a view. The PL/SQL compiler won't get confused, but you might, and your SQL statements inside PL/SQL might not work as intended. So you should always make sure that there is no ambiguity between SQL and PL/SQL identifiers. The best way to do this is to qualify all references to PL/SQL variables with their scope name.

### Example

Consider the following block:

```
CREATE OR REPLACE PROCEDURE show_fav_flavor (
    pref_type IN VARCHAR2)
IS
    pref VARCHAR2(100);
BEGIN
    SELECT preference INTO pref
      FROM personal_preferences PP
     WHERE PP.pref_type = pref_type;
    pl (pref);
END;
```

You might think that the WHERE clause restricts the query to only those rows where pref_type equals the value passed in through the parameter. In fact, it's no different logically than "1 = 1". SQL always takes precedence over PL/SQL when resolving identifiers.

There are two solutions to this problem:

- Use prefixes/suffixes on variable and parameter names to distinguish them from column and table names, as in:

```
CREATE OR REPLACE PROCEDURE show_fav_flavor (
    pref_type_in IN VARCHAR2)
```

- Always qualify references to PL/SQL elements inside the SQL statement, as in:

```
SELECT preference INTO pref
  FROM personal_preferences PP
 WHERE PP.pref_type = show_fav_flavor.pref_type;
```

I recommend the second approach. It requires more typing, but it's foolproof. With the first solution, for example, a DBA can conceivably add a column to the personal_preferences table called pref_type_in and completely muck up my code!

### Benefits

The behavior of your SQL statements will be predictable and consistent over time, regardless of changes to the underlying data structures.

### Challenges

You have to write more code, qualifying all references to those variables inside SQL.

For SQL inside anonymous blocks, you need to create a label for the block in the form <<*blockname*>> so you have a name to use inside the SQL statement.

## SQL-02: Use incremental COMMITs to avoid rollback segment errors when changing large numbers of rows.

It's very easy to issue an UPDATE statement that can (theoretically) change one million rows or 10 million rows. It's more of a challenge to get that statement to succeed without running out of rollback segment space. And these errors are often hard to predict, because they depend on the volume of data for a specific run.

If you have this problem, you should switch to incremental commits: issue a COMMIT statement every 1,000 or 10,000 rows—whatever level works for your rollback segments.

### Example

You can declare a counter variable and update the variable with each execution of the loop body. If you process data from within a cursor FOR loop, you can also take advantage of the built-in %ROWCOUNT attribute, as shown here:

```
DECLARE
    c_commit_plateau CONSTANT PLS_INTEGER := 10000;

    CURSOR my_cur
    IS
        SELECT *
          FROM my_table;
BEGIN
    FOR my_rec IN my_cur
    LOOP
        INSERT INTO temp_data VALUES (my_rec.id);

        IF (MOD (my_cur%rowcount, c_commit_plateau) = 0)
        THEN
            COMMIT WORK;
        END IF;
    END LOOP;

    COMMIT WORK;
END;
```

You can also build an API to the PL/SQL COMMIT statement that automatically handles incremental commits and adds value (logging, on-off toggles) to COMMIT. You can find an example of such a package in the PL/Vision library.

### Benefits

Make your code more robust by avoiding hard-to-predict rollback segment errors in your programs.

When you use %ROWCOUNT, there's no need to declare a local variable to keep count of how many records have been processed.

### Challenges

You need to identify potential problem areas in your code (far better than waiting until a program fails).

Calling the MOD function through every iteration of the loop is likely to be slower than checking the value of a counter.

### Resources

*plvcmt.sps* and *plvcmt.spb*: In the PL/Vision Lite version of the PLVcmt package.

---

## SQL-03: Use autonomous transactions to isolate the effect of COMMITs and ROLLBACKs (Oracle8i).

A new feature in Oracle8*i* called *autonomous transactions* allows you to make and save (or roll back) changes within a single PL/SQL block—without affecting the outer or main transaction.

To make a PL/SQL block an autonomous transaction, simply include this statement in the declaration section of the block:

```
PRAGMA AUTONOMOUS_TRANSACTION;
```

You can use this statement in any procedure and function and in any non-nested anonymous block.

### Example

```
CREATE OR REPLACE PROCEDURE log_error (
    code IN INTEGER, msg IN VARCHAR2)
AS
    PRAGMA AUTONOMOUS_TRANSACTION;
BEGIN
    INSERT INTO error_log
        (errcode, errtext, created_on, created_by)
    VALUES
        (code, msg, SYSDATE, USER);

    COMMIT;
EXCEPTION
    WHEN OTHERS THEN ROLLBACK;
END;
```

### Benefits

With autonomous transactions, you can write and save messages in an database log without affecting the main transaction.

You can execute from SQL PL/SQL functions that change the database.

You can write PL/SQL components or cartridges that behave nicely in a distributed computing environment.

### Resources

*log.pkg* and *log.tst*: A simple logging package that uses autonomous transactions, and a companion script you can use to test the functionality.

# Querying Data from PL/SQL

The best practices in this section apply when you are querying data from PL/SQL programs.

## SQL-04: Put single-row fetches inside functions; never hard-code a query in your block.

Always put your single-row query inside a function, and then call the function to return the information you need (whether it's a scalar value, an entire record, or even a collection) through the RETURN clause.

### Example

Instead of writing code like this:

```
BEGIN
    SELECT title INTO l_title    -- HARD-CODED
      FROM book                  -- QUERY...
     WHERE isbn =isbn_in;        -- BAD IDEA!
```

you should create a function, ideally within a "table encapsulation package":

```
PACKAGE te_book
IS
    FUNCTION title (isbn_in IN book.isbn%TYPE)
        RETURN book.title%TYPE;
```

Now your application code looks like this:

```
BEGIN
    l_title := te_book.title (isbn_in);
```

### Benefits

Optimal performance: The query is written once, presumably by the developer who best knows how to write it. Since there is a single physical representation of the query in code, the parsed version of the cursor is cached and used repeatedly.

Easy maintenance: If you need to change the query, you only have to do it in one place.

Consistent error handling: Individual developers don't have to remember to write handlers for NO_DATA_FOUND and TOO_MANY_ROWS.

### Challenges

Discipline is required in a multi-person team environment to ensure that the team has at least one person overseeing this type of encapsulation and that the whole team adheres to this standard.

There will be a larger volume of code to write and manage (your DBA must size the System Global Area accordingly). Explore the possibilities of generating these functions from the data dictionary.

## SQL-05: Hide reliance on the dual table.

This is a special case of **SQL-04** but is worth mentioning. The dual table is a "dummy" table that is used by Oracle itself and by many developers to access functionality in the SQL engine that is otherwise not available in PL/SQL.

Use of the dual table is, therefore (and by definition) a workaround or "kludge." We all know we have to do these things, but we also know or hope that over time, we will no longer have to do them. So hide your kludges behind a function or procedure and then, when they are no longer needed, you can change the implementation without affecting those usages.

### Example

Instead of:

```
DECLARE
    my_id INTEGER;
BEGIN
    SELECT patient_seq.NEXTVAL INTO my_id
      FROM dual;
```

you should build yourself a function:

```
CREATE OR REPLACE FUNCTION next_patient_id
    RETURN patient.patient_id%TYPE
IS
    retval patient.patient_id%TYPE;
BEGIN
    SELECT patient_seq.nextval
      INTO retval
      FROM dual;
    RETURN retval;
END;
```

And then you only need to write this to get your next primary key value:

```
DECLARE
    my_id INTEGER;
BEGIN
    my_id := next_patient_id;
```

### Benefits

You gain the ability to remove workarounds and kludges from code more easily as underlying software improves.

### Resources

*nextseq.sf*: A function that uses dynamic SQL to offer a single function that retrieves the *n*th NEXTVAL from any sequence you specify.

---

## SQL-06: Define multi-row cursors in packages so they can be used from multiple programs.

Create a package to hold all the multiple-row queries for a given business entity (which may be made up of one or more tables and views). You can then open, fetch, and close those cursors from multiple programs.

Here's an example of such a package:

```
PACKAGE book_pkg
IS
    CURSOR allbooks IS
        SELECT * FROM book;

    CURSOR books_by_category (
        category_in IN book.category%TYPE)
    IS
        SELECT * FROM book
         WHERE category = category_in;
```

and here is a use of a packaged cursor:

```
BEGIN
    OPEN book_pkg.books_by_category (
        'THRILLER');
    LOOP
        FETCH book_pkg.books_by_category
         INTO thrillers_rec;
         ...
    END LOOP;
    CLOSE book_pkg.books_by_category;
END;
```

### Benefits

Individual developers don't have to learn all the ins and outs of potentially complex, multijoin queries.

When changes to queries are required, you only have to go to one place in your code to make the fix.

### Challenges

Packaged cursors are persistent; they stay open until you explicitly close them or until you disconnect (unless you use the SERIALLY_REUSABLE pragma). This is different from locally declared cursors, which close automatically when the current block ends.

Team processes must be defined. Developers need to know where to go to find the code, whom to go to when it needs changing, and so on.

## SQL-07: *Fetch into cursor records, never into a hard-coded list of variables.*

Whenever you fetch data from a cursor, whether it's an explicit cursor or a cursor variable, you should fetch into a record defined from that cursor with %ROWTYPE.

### Example

Suppose I have declared a cursor in a package as follows:

```
PACKAGE book_pkg
IS
    CURSOR books_by_category (
        category_in IN book.category%TYPE)
    IS
        SELECT title, author FROM book
        WHERE category = category_in;
END book_pkg;
```

Now I want to fetch information from this cursor. If I fetch into individual variables like this:

```
DECLARE
    l_title book.title%TYPE;
    l_author book.author%TYPE;
BEGIN
    OPEN book_pkg.books_by_category ('SCIFI');
    FETCH book_pkg.books_by_category INTO
        l_title, l_author;
```

then I am hard-coding the number of values returned by a cursor, as well as the datatypes of the individual variables. (I could use %TYPE, but I am more likely to be lazy.)

This is a dangerous assumption to make. What if the owner of the book_pkg package decides to add another column to the SELECT list? My code will then fail to compile.

If, on the other hand, I write my code like this:

```
DECLARE
    scifi_rec book_pkg.books_by_category%ROWTYPE;
BEGIN
    OPEN book_pkg.books_by_category ('SCIFI');
    FETCH book_pkg.books_by_category INTO
        scifi_rec;
```

then, if the cursor ever changes, my code will/can be recompiled, and it will automatically adapt to the new cursor structure.

### Benefits

Code adapts automatically to changes in the underlying cursor structure.

You write less code, since you don't have to declare individual variables.

## SQL-08: *Use COUNT only when the actual number of occurrences is needed.*

Don't use the COUNT function to answer either of the following questions:

*   Is there at least one row matching certain criteria?
*   Is there more than one row matching certain criteria?

Instead, use an explicit cursor inside a function.

You should use COUNT only when you need to answer the question: "How *many* rows match a certain criteria?"

### Example

Suppose I have been asked to write a program that returns TRUE if there is at least one book in a given category. I could write it like this:

```
CREATE OR REPLACE FUNCTION atleastone (
    category_in IN book.category%TYPE)
    RETURN BOOLEAN
IS
    numbooks INTEGER;
BEGIN
    SELECT COUNT(*) INTO numbooks
      FROM book
     WHERE category = category_in;
    RETURN (numbooks > 0);
END;
```

But I am asking the RDBMS to do lots of unnecessary work. It might find, for instance, that there are 12 million books in the NON-FICTION category. A better approach is:

```
CREATE OR REPLACE FUNCTION atleastone (
    category_in IN book.category%TYPE)
    RETURN BOOLEAN
IS
    retval BOOLEAN;

    CURSOR category_cur
       SELECT 1
         FROM book
        WHERE category = category_in;
BEGIN
    OPEN category_cur;
    FETCH category_cur INTO category_rec;
    retval := category_cur%FOUND;
    CLOSE category_cur;
    RETURN retval;
END;
```

In other words: all I have to do is see if there is a single row, and I am done.

### Benefits

With this practice, you get optimal performance out of your query.

The readability of your code also improves, since it's a more accurate translation of the requirement.

### Challenges

You will write a bit more code, especially if you take the time to put your query inside a function, as recommended in **SQL-04**.

### Resources

*atleastone.sql*: A SQL*Plus script comparing different approaches to answering the question "Is there at least one employee in department 20?"

---

## SQL-09: Use a cursor FOR loop to fetch all rows in a cursor unconditionally.

The cursor FOR loop construct is a wonderful addition to the PL/SQL language, reflecting the tight integration between SQL and PL/SQL. Use it whenever you need to fetch every single row identified by the cursor, but don't use it if you have to conditionally exit from the loop.

### Example

I need to display the total number of books sold for each of my PL/SQL texts. That's easy:

```
DECLARE
   CURSOR sef_books_cur IS
      SELECT title, total_count
        FROM book_sales
       WHERE author = 'FEUERSTEIN, STEVEN';
BEGIN
   FOR rec IN sef_books_cur
   LOOP
      pl (rec.title || ': ' ||
         rec.total_count || ' copies');
   END LOOP;
END;
```

Perfect use of a cursor FOR loop! Suppose, on the other hand, the requirement was this: "Display all the books and their numbers sold until the total reaches 100,000; then quit." In this case, I should use a WHILE loop with an EXIT WHEN statement. Here's an example:

```
DECLARE
   total_sold  PLS_INTEGER := 0;

   CURSOR sef_books_cur IS
      SELECT title, total_count
        FROM book_sales
       WHERE author = 'FEUERSTEIN, STEVEN';

   rec  sef_books_cur%ROWTYPE;
stop_loop BOOLEAN;
BEGIN
   OPEN sef_books_cur;
```

```
    LOOP
       FETCH sef_books_cur INTO rec;
             stop_loop := sef_books_cur%NOTFOUND;
             IF NOT stop_loop
             THEN
                 pl (rec.title || ': ' ||
                 rec.total_count || ' copies');
             total_sold := total_sold + rec.total_count;
             stop_loop := total_sold >= 100000;
          END IF;
          EXIT WHEN stop_loop;
       END LOOP;
       CLOSE sef_books_cur;
    END;
```

### Benefits

The cursor FOR loop saves you coding effort and does more work for you—that is, it opens, fetches from, and closes the cursor.

The resulting code is very readable; use of the FOR loop says that you are fetching all rows from the cursor.

### Challenges

After the END LOOP statement, you can't tell anything about what happened inside the loop, such as: "Was anything actually retrieved?" or "How many rows were retrieved?" You have to add your own counters and variables inside the body of the loop to figure that out.

If a developer isn't careful, the body of code inside the cursor FOR loop can become very large. Since the FOR loop record isn't referenceable outside the loop, it may be hard to apply step-wise refinement with local modules to make the code more manageable. See **MOD-03** for more information about this technique.

---

## SQL-10: Never use a cursor FOR loop to fetch just one row.

If you have a single-row query, you can use a cursor FOR loop, but it's misleading. A cursor FOR loop is designed to fetch all (multiple) rows from a cursor. The only rationale for using a cursor FOR loop for a single-row query is that you don't have to write as much code, and that is both dubious and a lame excuse.

### Example

Doesn't this look silly:

```
CREATE OR REPLACE FUNCTION book_title (
    isbn_in IN book.isbn%TYPE)
RETURN book.title%TYPE
IS
    CURSOR title_cur IS
    SELECT title INTO l_title
      FROM book
     WHERE isbn =isbn_in;
```

```
    l_rec title_cur%ROWTYPE;
BEGIN
    FOR rec IN title_cur
    LOOP
        l_rec := rec;
    END LOOP;
    RETURN l_rec.title;
END;
```

Instead, use a SELECT INTO or explicit cursor; for example:

```
CREATE OR REPLACE FUNCTION book_title (
    isbn_in IN book.isbn%TYPE)
RETURN book.title%TYPE
IS
    CURSOR title_cur IS
    SELECT title INTO l_title
      FROM book
     WHERE isbn =isbn_in;

    l_rec title_cur%ROWTYPE;
BEGIN
    OPEN title_cur;
    FETCH title_cur INTO l_rec;
    CLOSE title_cur;
    RETURN l_rec.title;
END;
```

### Benefits

Your code doesn't look silly. It satisfies the requirement in the most direct and understandable way.

A cursor FOR loop is less efficient than either a SELECT INTO or an explicit cursor fetch.

### Resources

*explimpl.pkg* and *explimpl.sql*: Scripts that compare the performance of cursor FOR loops to other fetching methods for a single row.

## SQL-11: Specify columns to be updated in a SELECT FOR UPDATE statement.

Use the SELECT FOR UPDATE statement to request that locks be placed on all rows identified by the query. This is done when you know you will change some or all of those rows, and you don't want another session to change them out from under you.

Specify the columns to be updated so that (a) anyone reading the code knows the intentions of your program, and (b) if your query contains a join of more than one table, Oracle will lock only the rows in those tables that contain any of the specified columns.

### Example

The following code sets the favorite ice cream flavor of the Feuerstein family to
ROCKY ROAD, but doesn't lock any rows in the person table:

```
DECLARE
    CURSOR change_prefs_cur IS
        SELECT PER.name, PREF.name flavor
          FROM person PER, preference PREF
         WHERE PER.name = PREF.person_name
           AND PREF.type = 'ICE CREAM'
           FOR UPDATE OF PREF.name;
BEGIN
    FOR rec IN change_prefs_cur
    LOOP
       IF rec.name LIKE 'FEUERSTEIN%'
       THEN
          UPDATE preference SET name = 'ROCKY ROAD'
           WHERE CURRENT OF change_prefs_cur;
       END IF;
    END LOOP;
END;
/
```

### Benefits

You keep to a minimum the number of locks placed on rows in tables.

You self-document the behavior of your code, which is important for those who
come to your code later in its life to maintain it.

### Resources

*forupdate.sql*: Contains the code for the example in this section.

---

## SQL-12: Parameterize explicit cursors.

Cursors return information, just as functions do, and they can accept parameters
just as functions do (but only IN parameters). By defining your explicit cursors to
accept parameterized values, these cursors are more easily reused in different
circumstances and programs. This added value becomes most apparent when you
define cursors in package specifications.

### Example

Instead of this:

```
DECLARE
    CURSOR r_and_d_cur IS
        SELECT last_name FROM employee
         WHERE department_id = 10;
BEGIN
    OPEN r_and_d_cur;
```

move your cursor to a package:

```
CREATE OR REPLACE PACKAGE dept_info_pkg
IS
    CURSOR name_cur (dept IN INTEGER) IS
        SELECT last_name FROM employee
        WHERE department_id = dept;
```

and then open it like this:

```
BEGIN
    open dept_info_pkg.name_cur (10);
```

or, even better, do this to avoid the hard-coded literal:

```
DECLARE
    r_and_d_dept CONSTANT PLS_INTEGER := 10;
BEGIN
    open dept_info_pkg.name_cur (r_and_d_dept);
```

### Benefits

Application improvement is likely to improve, because parameters in a cursor are treated as bind variables. So, no matter what value is passed to the cursor, the SQL statement stays the same and isn't parsed repeatedly.

You will achieve higher levels of reuse in your application, reducing maintenance requirements.

## SQL-13: Use RETURNING to retrieve information about modified rows (Oracle8).

The RETURNING clause, available in Oracle8 and above, allows you to retrieve information from rows you have just modified with an INSERT, UPDATE, or DELETE statement. This clause allows you to perform—in a single operation—what you would previously have done in two operations (INSERT, then SELECT, for example).

### Example

Suppose that I am using a sequence to generate the primary key of the patient table in my universal health care system. I then need to use that new primary key for another operation. Prior to Oracle8, I would have written code like this:

```
INSERT INTO patient (patient_id, last_name, first_name)
    VALUES (patient_seq.NEXTVAL, 'FEUERSTEIN', 'STEVEN');

SELECT patient_id INTO l_patient_id
    FROM patient
WHERE last_name = 'FEUERSTEIN';
```

or even like this:

```
SELECT patient_seq.NEXTVAL INTO l_patient_id
    FROM dual;

INSERT INTO patient (patient_id, last_name, first_name)
    VALUES (l_patient_id, 'FEUERSTEIN', 'STEVEN');
```

With RETURNING, I can collapse two statements into a single INSERT statement:

```
INSERT INTO patient (patient_id, last_name, first_name)
   VALUES (patient_seq.NEXTVAL, 'FEUERSTEIN', 'STEVEN')
   RETURNING patient_id INTO l_patient_id;
```

You can also use the RETURNING clause in dynamic SQL and FORALL statements to obtain information about multiple rows affected by DML statements.

### Benefits

You will see improved performance in your applications.

Code volume will be reduced.

### Challenges

Your code will not run in versions of Oracle prior to Oracle8.

### Resources

*returning.tst*: A script comparing the performance of INSERT-SELECT to INSERT-RETURNING.

## SQL-14: Use BULK COLLECT to improve performance of multi-row queries (Oracle8i).

Recognizing that you often need to return large numbers of rows from the database, Oracle8*i* offers a new BULK COLLECT clause for queries. When you use BULK COLLECT, you retrieve multiple rows of data in a single request to the RDBMS. The data is then deposited into a series of collections.

### Example

To use BULK COLLECT, you need to declare collections to hold all the retrieved data. Then, preface your INTO clause with the BULK COLLECT keywords, and you are done:

```
CREATE OR REPLACE PROCEDURE process_employees
    (deptno_in IN dept.deptno%TYPE)
RETURN emplist_t
IS
   TYPE numTab IS TABLE OF emp.empno%TYPE;
   TYPE charTab IS TABLE OF emp.ename%TYPE;
   TYPE dateTab IS TABLE OF emp.hiredate%TYPE;
   enos numTab;
   names charTab;
   hdates dateTab;
BEGIN
   SELECT empno, ename, hiredate
      BULK COLLECT INTO enos, names, hdates
      FROM emp
      WHERE deptno = deptno_in;
   ...
END process_employees;
```

Or, if you are using an explicit cursor:

```
BEGIN
    OPEN emp_cur INTO emp_rec;
    FETCH emp_cur BULK COLLECT INTO enos, names, hdates;
```

### Benefits

You will see an improvement (in some cases, a dramatic improvement) in query performance.

### Challenges

You must declare a separate collection for each element in the SELECT list.

You must be careful when the SELECT returns many thousands of rows. There could be many users running the same program in a session, which can lead to memory problems. Try to restrict the bulk collection by using ROWNUM, for instance.

# Changing Data from PL/SQL

With PL/SQL, you can not only query information from an underlying Oracle database but also change data in tables with the INSERT, UPDATE, and DELETE operations.

## SQL-15: Encapsulate INSERT, UPDATE, and DELETE statements behind procedure calls.

Write a standalone procedure or put such procedures inside a single "table encapsulation package," but never, ever embed DML statements directly within application code.

---

### Know Thy SQL

Take the "Know Thy SQL" test: pick a table, any critical table in your application schema. Ask yourself this question: "Do I know where all or any of the INSERT statements for this table appear in my code?" Chances are that you can't answer definitively, and that is because we PL/SQL developers are somewhat haphazard about managing our SQL statements. The result? Tremendous obstacles to performing accurate impact analysis on your code from database changes, among other things.

---

### Example

Instead of writing an INSERT as follows:

```
INSERT INTO book (
    isbn, title, author)
VALUES (
```

```
'1-56592-675-7',
'Oracle PL/SQL Programming Guide to Oracle8i Features',
'Feuerstein, Steven');
```

use a standalone procedure, as in:

```
add_book (
    '1-56592-675-7',
    'Oracle PL/SQL Programming Guide to Oracle8i Features',
    'Feuerstein, Steven');
```

or a packaged procedure:

```
te_book.ins (
    '1-56592-675-7',
    'Oracle PL/SQL Programming Guide to Oracle8i Features',
    'Feuerstein, Steven');
```

### Benefits

Your application runs faster. All programs that perform inserts into a given table use exactly the same INSERT, which results in less parsing and reduced demands on SGA memory.

Your application handles DML-related errors consistently. It's not up to individual developers to write error-logging mechanisms or decide how to deal with particular errors.

### Challenges

You need to write or generate more procedural code.

Your DBA may need to adjust the size of the shared pool area to handle the increased volume of code.

You may need to create multiple update procedures, to match up with various combinations of columns that you update in your application.

### Resources

*te_employee.pks* and *te_employee.pkb*: Examples of the specification and body of a table encapsulation package.

---

## SQL-16: Reference cursor attributes immediately after executing the SQL operation.

INSERT, UPDATE, and DELETE statements are all executed as "implicit cursors" in PL/SQL. You don't, in other words, explicitly declare, open, and process these kinds of statements. You simply issue the INSERT, UPDATE, or DELETE statement, and the underlying Oracle SQL engine takes care of the cursor management.

You can obtain information about the results of the implicit operation most recently executed in your session by checking any of the following cursor attributes:

| Attribute | Returns |
|-----------|---------|
| SQL%ROWCOUNT | Number of rows affected by the DML statement |
| SQL%ISOPEN | Always FALSE, since the cursor is opened and then closed implicitly |
| SQL%FOUND | Returns TRUE if the statement affects at least one row |
| SQL%NOTFOUND | Returns FALSE if the statement affects at least one row |

There is only one set of SQL% attributes in a session; they always reflect the last implicit operation performed. You should, therefore, keep to an absolute minimum the code that falls between the DML operation and the attribute reference. Otherwise, the value returned by the attribute might not correspond to the desired SQL statement, resulting in hard-to-resolve bugs.

### Example

I have the good fortune to have published eight books with O'Reilly & Associates on the subject of PL/SQL. Let's suppose that all my titles contain the word "PL/SQL" (and that all O'Reilly books with PL/SQL in the title were written or co-written by yours truly). We have decided to change the font size in the books to cut the page count in half and now need to update the database:

```
DECLARE
   PROCEDURE show_max_count
   IS
      l_total_pages PLS_INTEGER;
   BEGIN
      SELECT MAX (page_count)
         INTO l_total_pages
         FROM book
         WHERE title LIKE '%PL/SQL%';
      DBMS_OUTPUT.PUT_LINE (l_total_pages);
   END;
BEGIN
   UPDATE book SET page_count = page_count / 2
    WHERE title LIKE '%PL/SQL%';

   show_max_count;

   DBMS_OUTPUT.PUT_LINE (
      'Pages adjusted in ' || SQL%ROWCOUNT || ' books.');
END;
```

My intention in this program is to display the number of books that have been updated. Between my UPDATE and my reference to SQL%ROWCOUNT, I call a procedure (show_max_count) that executes an implicit SELECT MAX. The reference to SQL%ROWCOUNT will, therefore, reflect the outcome of the SELECT rather than the UPDATE.

## SQL-17: Check SQL%ROWCOUNT when updating or removing data that "should" be there.

The SQL%ROWCOUNT cursor attribute returns the numbers of rows affected by the most recent INSERT, UPDATE, or DELETE statement executed in your session. Check this value to verify that the action completed properly. (Note that updates and deletes don't raise an exception if no rows are affected.)

### Example

Let's suppose that the local library spelled my name incorrectly when they entered my books into their system. Now they need to fix it and they want to make sure they got them all (eight, including this text):

```
BEGIN
    UPDATE book
        SET author = 'FEUERSTEIN, STEVEN'
     WHERE author = 'FEVERSTEIN, STEPHEN';

    IF SQL%ROWCOUNT < 8
    THEN
        ROLLBACK;
        Pl (
           'Find the rest of his books, rapido!');
    END IF;
END;
```

### Benefits

Your programs will check for and be able to handle problems more effectively.

## SQL-18: Use FORALL to improve performance of collection-based DML (Oracle8i).

Recognizing that you often need to modify (insert, delete, or update) large numbers of rows in the database from within PL/SQL, Oracle8i offers a new FORALL statement. This statement can dramatically improve your DML performance by reducing the number of "context switches" between the PL/SQL statement executor and the SQL engine.

Consider using FORALL whenever you perform a DML operation within a loop.

### Example

The following cursor FOR loop performs many individual row updates:

```
BEGIN
    FOR book_rec IN book_pkg.book_cur
    LOOP
        UPDATE borrowings
            SET borrow_date = SYSDATE
                borrower_id = book_rec.user_id
          WHERE isbn = book_rec.isbn;
    END LOOP;
END;
```

Now I use FORALL to accomplish the same thing, but with a single pass to the SQL engine and RDBMS:

```
DECLARE
    TYPE books_t IS TABLE OF borrower.user_id%TYPE;
    books books_t := books_t();
    TYPE isbns_t IS TABLE OF book.isbn%TYPE;
    isbns isbns _t := isbns_t();
BEGIN
    FOR book_rec IN book_pkg.book_cur
    LOOP
        books.EXTEND;
        isbns.EXTEND;
        books(books.LAST) := book_rec.user_id;
        isbns(isbns.LAST) := book_rec.isbn;
    END LOOP;

    FORALL indx IN books.FIRST .. books.LAST
        UPDATE borrowings
            SET borrow_date = SYSDATE
                borrower_id = books(indx)
            WHERE isbn = isbns(indx);
END;
```

Notice that I still need the cursor FOR loop to populate my collections. The time it takes to do this, however, is usually more than offset by the improvements in UPDATE processing.

### Benefits

You can significantly improve the performance of multirow DML operations.

If an error occurs during the DML activity, any statements that have already been processed aren't rolled back. This is great if you want to preserve any changes that "got through."

### Challenges

You may have to convert your programs to populate collections, which are then passed to the FORALL statement.

If an error occurs during the DML activity, any statements that have already been processed aren't rolled back. This is a problem if you wanted "all or nothing" for your DML.

### Resources

*bulktiming.sql*: A script to compare performance of row-by-row DML and FORALL-based DML.

# Dynamic SQL and Dynamic PL/SQL

"Dynamic" means that the SQL statement or PL/SQL block that you execute is constructed, parsed, and compiled at runtime, not at the time the code is compiled. Dynamic SQL offers a tremendous amount of flexibility—but also complexity.

With Oracle8*i* and above, you can use *native dynamic SQL* (NDS) to take care of dynamic SQL. Prior to Oracle8*i*, you must rely on the DBMS_SQL built-in package.

## SQL-19: Encapsulate dynamic SQL parsing to improve error detection and cleanup.

Dynamic SQL is tricky; you generally glue together different chunks of text (with the concatenation operator) to form what you hope is a valid SQL or PL/SQL statement. Either through programmer error or user error, you can end up with a bad chunk of SQL, resulting in a parse error.

To identify and fix these errors, you should create your own parsing "engine" on top of DBMS_SQL.PARSE and the NDS statements. This program traps and displays error information, and cleans up any cursors.

### Example

This technique is most crucial for DBMS_SQL. Don't ever call DBMS_SQL.PARSE directly in your program. Instead, call your own parse encapsulator. Why would you bother to do this? Consider the following block of code. It leaves a DBMS_SQL cursor unclosed and unclosable; you need to be able to reference the dyncur variable in the call to DBMS_SQL.CLOSE_CURSOR, but that variable is erased once the exception is propagated:

```
DECLARE
    dyncur PLS_INTEGER := DBMS_SQL.open_cursor;
BEGIN
    -- Whoops, forget the FROM clause!
    DBMS_SQL.parse (
        dyncur, 'select * dual', DBMS_SQL.native);
END;
```

Here's a very simple example of an encapsulation for DBMS_SQL.PARSE:

```
CREATE OR REPLACE FUNCTION open_and_parse (
    dynsql_in IN VARCHAR2,
    dbms_mode_in IN INTEGER := NULL)
RETURN INTEGER
IS
    dyncur INTEGER;
BEGIN
    dyncur := DBMS_SQL.OPEN_CURSOR;
    DBMS_SQL.PARSE (dyncur, dynsql_in,
        NVL (dbms_mode_in, DBMS_SQL.NATIVE));

    RETURN dyncur;
EXCEPTION
    WHEN OTHERS
    THEN
        DBMS_SQL.CLOSE_CURSOR (dyncur);
        pl (SQLERRM);
        pl (dynsql_in);
        RETURN NULL;
END;
/
```

See the "Resources" section for a more comprehensive solution with DBMS_SQL.

Here's the native dynamic SQL equivalent:

```
CREATE OR REPLACE PROCEDURE exec_immed (
    dynsql_in IN VARCHAR2)
    AUTHID CURRENT_USER
IS
BEGIN
    EXECUTE IMMEDIATE dynsql_in;
EXCEPTION
    WHEN OTHERS
    THEN
        pl (SQLERRM)
        pl (dynsql_in);
END;
/
```

### Benefits

You can identify and fix errors in your program, or train your users to use the interface to your dynamic SQL, more effectively.

You will not inadvertently leave open DBMS_SQL cursors that are unclosable in your session.

### Challenges

With DBMS_SQL (prior to Oracle8*i*), any SQL statement passed to open_and_parse is parsed under the privileges of the owner of open_and_parse. You should, therefore, install this program in every schema that wants to use it. Or, if you are running Oracle8*i* and still using DBMS_SQL, use the AUTHID CURRENT_USER clause to ensure that the program runs under the invoker's authority.

With NDS, you can't separate the parse and execute phases; it's all done by EXECUTE IMMEDIATE. That makes it hard to write a truly generic program to handle any SQL string (you have to account for the USING and INTO clauses). The general principle still applies, however: *trap, handle, and display dynamic SQL errors!*

### Resources

*openprse.pkg*: A package that allocates new DBMS_SQL cursors only when necessary, and displays SQLERRM and the SQL string if a parse error occurs.

---

## SQL-20: Bind, do not concatenate, variable values into dynamic SQL strings.

When you bind a variable value into a dynamic SQL string, you insert a "placeholder" into the string. This allows Oracle to parse a "generic" version of that SQL statement, which can be used over and over again, regardless of the actual value of the variable, without repeated parsing.

On the other hand, if you concatenate, then every time the value you concatenate changes, the physical SQL statement changes, causing excessive parsing.

You can bind only *variable values*. You can't bind in the names of tables or columns, nor can you bind in parts of a SQL statement structure, such as the entire WHERE clause. In these cases, you must use concatenation.

## Example

Here's an example of binding with DBMS_SQL. This program updates any numeric column in the specified table, based on the supplied name:

```
CREATE OR REPLACE PROCEDURE updnumval (
    tab_in IN VARCHAR2,
    namecol_in IN VARCHAR2,
    numcol_in IN VARCHAR2,
    name_in IN VARCHAR2,
    val_in IN NUMBER)
IS
    cur PLS_INTEGER;
    fdbk PLS_INTEGER;
BEGIN
    cur := open_and_parse (
        'UPDATE ' || tab_in ||
          ' SET ' || numcol_in || ' = :val
        WHERE ' || namecol_in || ' LIKE :name');

    DBMS_SQL.BIND_VARIABLE (cur, 'val', val_in);
    DBMS_SQL.BIND_VARIABLE (cur, 'name', name_in);

    fdbk := DBMS_SQL.EXECUTE (cur);

    DBMS_SQL.CLOSE_CURSOR (cur);
END;
/
```

Here's one possible usage of this procedure:

```
SQL> exec updnumval ('emp', 'ename', 'sal', 'S%', 5000)
```

## Benefits

Your System Global Area requires less memory for the dynamic SQL cursors.

Application performance improves due to reduced parsing.

You will find it easier and less bug-prone to write dynamic SQL code.

## Resources

*updnval2.pro*: Implementation of the updnumval program using concatenation so that you can compare the complexity of the implementations.

*effdsql.tst*: A script that allows you to compare performance of repetitive parsing using concatenation with a single parse that relies on binding instead.

## SQL-21: Soft-code the maximum length of columns in DBMS_ SQL.DEFINE_COLUMN calls.

When you call DBMS_SQL.DEFINE_COLUMN to define a VARCHAR2 column, you must provide the maximum length of the string that will be passed back to your program. Ideally, we'd use an attribute like %COLLEN to automatically draw that value from the data dictionary. There is, unfortunately, no such attribute. As a consequence, we usually sigh and hard-code a maximum length.

Rather than do that, create a package specification and place all column lengths you need to reference there. This way, if those lengths change, you can update just the one package. You can also generate this package specification directly from the data dictionary (see the "Resources" section).

### Example

I create a "column length" package:

```
CREATE OR REPLACE PACKAGE collen
IS
    city CONSTANT INTEGER := 15;
    state CONSTANT INTEGER := 2;
END collen;
```

And I now reference those constants whenever I call DBMS_SQL.DEFINE COLUMN:

```
DBMS_SQL.DEFINE_COLUMN (
    cursor_handle, 1, city, collen.city);

DBMS_SQL.DEFINE_COLUMN (
    cursor_handle, 2, state, collen.state);
```

### Benefits

You avoid hard-coding column lengths. If a column length changes, you update the value only in the package of named constants.

### Challenges

You have to build and maintain the column length package(s). Code generation will make the difference here.

### Resources

*genlenpkg.pro*: A program that generates the column length package for the specified table (VARCHAR2 columns only). Here's an example of the output from the genlenpkg procedure:

```
SQL> exec genlenpkg ('employee')
CREATE OR REPLACE PACKAGE employee$collen AS
    LAST_NAME CONSTANT PLS_INTEGER := 15;
    FIRST_NAME CONSTANT PLS_INTEGER := 15;
    MIDDLE_INITIAL CONSTANT PLS_INTEGER := 1;
    ENAME CONSTANT PLS_INTEGER := 30;
```

```
       CREATED_BY CONSTANT PLS_INTEGER := 100;
       CHANGED_BY CONSTANT PLS_INTEGER := 100;
   END PACKAGE employee$collen;
```

## SQL-22: Apply the invoker rights method to all stored code that executes dynamic SQL (Oracle8i).

Whenever you create a stored program (standalone or within a package) that parses a dynamic SQL statement, you should define that program with the "invoker rights" model. This is done by adding the following clause to the program header:

```
AUTHID CURRENT_USER
```

This feature is available only in Oracle8*i* and above. This clause ensures that the dynamic SQL string is parsed under the authority of the schema currently running the program, which is almost always the desired behavior.

### Example

If I were to create a reusable program to execute any DDL statement, I would make certain it used the AUTHID statement as follows:

```
CREATE OR REPLACE PROCEDURE runddl (
     ddl_in in VARCHAR2)
     AUTHID CURRENT_USER
IS
BEGIN
     EXECUTE IMMEDIATE ddl_in;
EXCEPTION
     WHEN OTHERS
     THEN
          pl (SQLERRM)
          pl (ddl_in);
          RAISE;
END;
/
```

### Benefits

You can build and share generic dynamic SQL utilities more easily. Developers don't have to worry about which schema owns the utility and whether or not the requested operation will affect someone else's schema.

### Challenges

This feature is available only in Oracle8*i*.

### Resources

*runddl.pro* and *runddl81.pro*: Generic DDL engine in both DBMS_SQL and NDS.

## SQL-23: Format dynamic SQL strings so they can be easily read and maintained.

When building long and possibly complex dynamic SQL statements, you should apply the same formatting rules as are applied to static code.

These strings are often the result of multiple concatenations, so they start off being less readable than static code. Don't compound the problem by treating this dynamic SQL as simply a set of concatenated strings. Consider it, instead, as a "program" in and of itself and format it—as much as possible—in the same way.

Many experienced dynamic SQL developers build a "typical" query or block (expressing the pattern of code they want to run dynamically), and then turn it into a string, with all the linebreaks and indentation intact.

### Example

Here's an example of well-formatted PL/SQL code: my very long string is broken into individual pieces so that it can be indented nicely. This formatting also, unfortunately, pleads ignorant to recognizing the significance of that string's contents:

```
DECLARE
   v_sql   VARCHAR2 (32767);
BEGIN
   v_sql :=
      'DECLARE CURSOR curs_get_orders IS ' ||
         ' SELECT * FROM ord_order; BEGIN ' ||
         ' FOR v_order_rec IN curs_get_orders LOOP ' ||
         ' process_order(v_order_rec.order_id); ' ||
         ' END LOOP; END;';
      EXECUTE IMMEDIATE v_sql;
END;
/
```

Here are two alternative formattings of the same assignment. In the first, I continue to use concatenation, but I break up the string and use indentation to present the block of code according to my usual conventions. In the second example, I write my block as a single string with embedded carriage returns displayed, to make sure it compiles correctly:

```
v_sql :=
   'DECLARE '
||    'CURSOR curs_get_orders IS '
||       'SELECT * FROM ord_order; '
|| 'BEGIN '
||    'FOR v_order_rec IN curs_get_orders LOOP '
||       'process_order(v_order_rec.order_id); '
||    'END LOOP; '
|| 'END;';

v_sql :=
   'DECLARE
      CURSOR curs_get_orders IS
         SELECT *
            FROM ord_order;
   BEGIN
```

```
        FOR v_order_rec IN curs_get_orders LOOP
           process_order(v_order_rec.order_id);
        END LOOP;
     END';
```

## Benefits

You can read and maintain the code much more easily.

## Challenges

It's extremely important to agree upon a standard approach within your team to formatting dynamic SQL strings. You might otherwise have different developers inserting different amounts and kinds of whitespace into dynamic SQL strings, resulting in unnecessary reparsing of logically equivalent cursors.

# 7

# *Program Construction*

There are three kinds of programs (also known as *modules*) in PL/SQL:

*Procedure*
> A procedure is a program that executes one or more statements. It's called as a standalone statement.

*Function*
> A function is a program that executes one or more statements and returns a value. It's called within an expression (assignment statement, conditional expression, etc.).

*Trigger*
> A trigger is a program whose execution is "triggered" by some event, usually a SQL operation on a table or column within a table.

All of these are named, executable code units. A package, as described in Chapter 8, *Package Construction*, is a container for procedures and/or functions, as well as data. Packages, therefore, aren't executable objects themselves.

## Structure and Parameters

The best practices in this section offer advice on how to structure your program units and how best to design parameter lists.

## *MOD-01: Encapsulate and name business rules and formulas behind function headers.*

This is one of the most important best practices you will ever read—and, I hope, follow. The one aspect of any software project that never changes is that stuff always changes. Business requirements, data structures, user interfaces: all these things change and change frequently. Your job as a programmer is to write code that adapts easily to these changes.

So whenever you need to express a business rule (such as, "Is this string a valid ISBN?"), put it inside a subroutine that hides the individual steps (which might change) and returns the results (if any).

And whenever you need a formula (such as, "the total fine for an overdue book is the number of days overdue times $.50"), express that formula inside its own function.

### Example

Suppose that you must be at least 10 years old to borrow books from the library. This is a simple formula and very unlikely to change. I set about building the application by creating the following trigger:

```
CREATE OR REPLACE TRIGGER are_you_too_young
    AFTER insert OR update
    ON borrower FOR EACH ROW
BEGIN
    IF :new.date_of_birth >
         ADD_MONTHS (SYSDATE, -12 * 10)
    THEN
      RAISE_APPLICATION_ERROR (
         -20703,
         'Borrower must be at least 10 yrs old.');
    END IF;
END;
/
```

Later, while building a batch-processing script that checks and loads over 10,000 borrower applications, I include the following check in the program:

```
BEGIN
    ...
    IF ADD_MONTHS (SYSDATE, -122) > rec.date_of_birth
    THEN
       err.log ('Borrower ' || rec.borrower_id ||
          ' is not ten years old.');
    ELSE
       ...load the data
```

And so on from there. I am left, unfortunately, with a real job on my hands when I get a memo that says: "The minimum age for a library card has been changed from 10 to 8 in order to support a new city-wide initiative to increase literacy." And then, of course, there are also the two bugs I introduced into my second construction of the rule. Did you notice them and the inconsistent error messages? The IF statement should read:

```
IF ADD_MONTHS (SYSDATE, -120) < rec.date_of_birth
```

If only I had created a simple function the first time I needed to calculate minimum valid age! Something like this:

```
CREATE OR REPLACE FUNCTION borrower_old_enough (
   dob_in IN DATE)
   RETURN BOOLEAN
IS
BEGIN
   RETURN NVL (
      dob_in < ADD_MONTHS (SYSDATE, -10 * 12),
      FALSE
      );
END;
```

And now I even check for a NULL value, which I forgot to do in those other programs.

### Benefits

You can update business rules and formulas in your code about as quickly and as often as users change everything that was supposedly "cast in stone." Developers apply those rules consistently throughout the application base, since they are simply calling a program.

Your code is much easier to understand, since developers don't have to wade through complex logic to understand which business rule is being implemented.

### Challenges

It's mostly a matter of discipline and advance planning. Before you start building your application, create a set of packages to hold business rules and formulas for distinct areas of functionality. Make sure that the names of the packages clearly identify their purpose. Then promote and use them rigorously throughout the development organization.

---

## MOD-02: Standardize module structure using function and procedure templates.

Once you adopt a set of guidelines for how developers should write procedures and functions, you need to help those developers follow their best practices. The bottom line is that guidelines will be followed if you make it easier to follow them than to ignore them.

For module standards, you can use either of the following approaches:

- Create a static template file that contains the generic logical structure for a procedure and/or function. Developers then copy that file to their own file, "de-genericize" the template by performing search and replace operations on placeholder strings with their own specific values (such as table names), and modify it from there.

- Use a program (one that you've written or a commercially available tool) that generates the code you want. This approach can be more flexible and can save you time, depending on how sophisticated a generator you use/create.

## Example

Here's a simple function template that reinforces the single RETURN recommendation (**MOD-07**) and encourages a standard header and consistent exception handling:

```
CREATE OR REPLACE FUNCTION <name> (
    <parm>_in IN <datatype>
)
    RETURN <datatype>
/*
|| STANDARD COPYRIGHT STATEMENT HERE
|| Author:
||   File:
*/
IS
    retval <datatype> := <default value>;;
BEGIN
    -- Put your code here

    RETURN retval;
EXCEPTION
    WHEN OTHERS
    THEN
        err.handle;
END <name>;
```

And here's an example that uses PLVgen (the code generation package from PL/Vision) to generate a standard function for a numeric datatype:

```
SQL> exec PLVgen.func ('total_pages', 1);
CREATE OR REPLACE FUNCTION total_pages
    RETURN NUMBER
/*
|| Program: total_pages
|| Author: null
||   File: total_pages.SQL
|| Created: November 16, 2000 15:57:03
||
|| Modification History:
|| Date      Who     Description
|| --------- ------- ---------------------
*/
IS
    retval NUMBER := NULL;
BEGIN
    PLVxmn.trace ('total_pages',
        PLVxmn.l_start, 'Starting program');

    /* Your executable code here... */

    PLVxmn.trace ('total_pages',
```

```
        PLVxmn.l_end, 'Ending program');

    RETURN retval;

EXCEPTION
    /* Call PLVexc in every handler. */
    WHEN OTHERS
    THEN
        PLVexc.recNgo;
        RETURN NULL;
END total_pages;
/
```

 One might argue that it's overkill to put trace calls (PLVxmn.trace) into such a simple function. You need to decide, on a case-by-case basis, which functions can and should absorb the tracing overhead. In PLVgen, you can set a switch to turn off inclusion of these calls.

### Benefits

The quality of each individual program is higher, since it's more likely to conform to best practices.

Programs are more consistent across the team and therefore easier to maintain and enhance.

### Challenges

First, you must decide on your basic formats, including standards for error handling. Then, you can either create template files or a basic code generator. Make doubly sure they are correct. Can you check whether they are being used? Can source code be auto-validated to check whether developers are altering the basic framework?

### Resources

*template.fun* and *template.pro*: Function and procedure template files.

*genmods.pkg*: A simple prototype of a function generator.

## MOD-03: Limit execution section sizes to a single page using modularization.

Sure, you're laughing out loud. You write code for the real world. It's really complicated. Fifty or sixty lines? You're lucky if your programs are less than 500 lines! Well, it's not a matter of complexity; it's more an issue of how you handle that complexity.

If your executable sections go on for hundreds of lines, with a loop starting on page 2 and ending on page 6 and so on, you will have a hard time "grasping the whole" and following the logic of the program.

An alternative is to use step-wise refinement (a.k.a. "top down decomposition"): don't dive into all the details immediately. Instead, start with a general description (written in actual code, mind you) of what your program is supposed to do. Then implement all subprogram calls in that description following the same method.

The result is that at any given level (PL/SQL block) of refinement, you can take in and easily comprehend the full underlying logic at that level. This technique is also referred to as "divide and conquer."

## Example

Consider the following procedure. The entire program might be hundreds of lines long, but the main body of assign_workload (starting with BEGIN /*main*/) is only 15 lines long. Not only that, I can read it pretty much as an exciting novel: "For every telesales rep, if that person's case load is less than their department's average, assign the next open case to that person and schedule the next appointment for that case."

```
CREATE OR REPLACE PROCEDURE assign_workload
IS
/* Overview: For every telesales rep, if that person's case load is less
than their department's average, assign the next open case to that person
and schedule the next appointment for that case. */
   ... declarations of cursors and variables

   -- Local module declarations of full programs
   PROCEDURE assign_next_open_case (
      telesales_id_in IN NUMBER, case_out OUT NUMBER)
   IS BEGIN
   ... full, local implementation;
   END assign_next_open_case;

   FUNCTION next_appointment (case_in IN NUMBER)
      RETURN DATE ... END next_appointment;

   PROCEDURE schedule_case (case_in IN NUMBER,
      date_in IN DATE) ... END schedule_case;

BEGIN /*main*/
   FOR telesales_rec IN telesales_cur
   LOOP
      IF analysis.caseload (
            telesales_rec.telesales_id) <
         analysis.avg_cases (
            telesales_rec.department_id);
      THEN
         assign_next_open_case (
            telesales_rec.telesales_id, case#);
         schedule_case (
            case#, next_appointment (case#));
      END IF;
   END LOOP;
END assign_workload;
```

### Benefits

You can implement complicated functionality with a minimum number of bugs by using step-wise refinement. Local modules and packaged programs play a major role in keeping each executable section small.

A developer can understand and maintain a program with confidence if he can read and grasp the logic of the code.

### Challenges

You have to be disciplined about holding off writing the low-level implementation of functionality. Instead, come up with accurate, descriptive names for packages, procedures, and functions that contain the implementations themselves.

### Resources

*http://www.construx.com*: Contains lots of good advice on writing modular code.

---

## MOD-04: Use named notation to clarify, self-document, and simplify module calls.

PL/SQL allows you to specify the name of a parameter along with its value in a parameter list by using this format:

```
parameter name => value
```

This is called *named notation*. With named notation, you can change the order in which you supply arguments; you can also skip over IN arguments with default values.

Use named notation whenever you make a call to a program that has any of the following characteristics:

- It has a long, confusing parameter list.

- It's used infrequently, meaning that there is little familiarity with it or its parameter list.

- It has default values for multiple IN parameters.

- In some cases, it actually requires named notation due to the parameter list design of overloaded programs (as is necessary with the built-in package, DBMS_OBFUSCATION_TOOLKIT).

### Example

Here's a procedure call that relies solely on *positional notation* (the default in PL/SQL):

```
IF perform_insert
THEN
   PLGdoir.ins (
      drv,
      c_table,
      NVL (aname, c_global),
      NVL (atype, c_global),
      text_in,
```

```
        v_info
    );
END IF;
```

I wrote that code, but I sure can't remember which parameter is going to get set to text_in. Here's another call to the same program:

```
IF v_tab = c_global
THEN
    PLGdoir.ins (
        driver_in => drv,
        objtype_in => c_table,
        attrname_in => c_global,
        attrtype_in => c_global,
        infotype_in => text_in,
        info_in => v_info
    );
```

Now I don't have to wonder; the code tells me exactly what is going on.

### Benefits

You will experience a dramatic improvement in the readability of the program calls inside your code.

Named notation also offers greater flexibility in how you construct your parameter lists.

### Challenges

You need to know or look up the names of arguments. For this reason, I can't support a recommendation of always using named notation. It would be most useful, on the other hand, if tools that generate code automatically follow named notation to enhance readability.

### Resources

*namednot.sql*: A file that demonstrates the different ways you can use named and positional notation to invoke a procedure.

---

## MOD-05: Avoid side-effects in your programs.

Build lots of individual programs, preferably inside packages. Design each program so that it has a single, clearly defined purpose. That purpose should, of course, be expressed in the program's name, as well as in the program header.

Avoid throwing extraneous functionality inside a program. Such statements are called "side-effects" and can cause lots of problems for people using your code—which means your code won't get used, except perhaps as source for a cut-and-paste session (or—in hard-copy form—for kindling).

### Example

Here's a program that by name and "core" functionality displays information about all books published within a certain date range:

```
CREATE OR REPLACE PROCEDURE display_book_info (
    start_in IN DATE,
```

```
        end_in IN DATE)
 IS
    CURSOR book_cur
    IS
        SELECT *
          FROM book
          WHERE date_published BETWEEN start_in
                      AND end_in;
 BEGIN
    FOR book_rec IN book_cur
    LOOP
        pl (book_rec.title || ' by ' ||
               book_rec.author);
        usage_analysis.update_borrow_history (
           book_rec);
    END LOOP;
 END display_book_info;
```

Notice, however, that it also updates the borrowing history for that book. Now, it might well be that at this point in time the display_book_info procedure is called only when the borrowing history also needs to be updated, justifying to some extent the way this program is written.

However, regardless of current requirements, the name of the program is clearly misleading; there is no way to know that display_book_info also updates borrowing history. This is a hidden side-effect, and one that can cause serious problems over time.

### Benefits

Your code can be used with greater confidence, since it does only what it says (via its name, for the most part) it's going to do. Developers will call and combine single-purpose programs as needed to get their job done.

## MOD-06: Use NOCOPY to minimize overhead when collections and records are [IN] OUT parameters (Oracle8i).

When you pass arguments through the parameter list of a program, those arguments can be passed by reference or by value:

- *By reference* means that the data structure manipulated inside the program points to the same location in memory that holds the value of the argument.
- *By value* means that the value of the argument is copied into the data structure of the program, and then copied back out to the argument data structure if no exception occurs.

Parameter passing in PL/SQL by default follows these rules:

- IN arguments are passed by reference.
- OUT and IN OUT arguments are passed by value.

This means that when you pass a large data structure (such as a collection, a record, or an instance of an object type) as an OUT or IN OUT parameter, your application can experience performance and memory degradation due to all this copying.

If you experience such degradation, you can consider two options:

- Use the Oracle8*i* NOCOPY hint to ask the PL/SQL compiler to not make a copy of your data structure.

- "Globalize" the data structure, so that instead of passing that large, complex structure as an argument, you reference it directly within the program.

### Example

Here's a parameter list that uses the NOCOPY hint for both of its IN OUT arguments:

```
PROCEDURE analyze_results (
    date_in IN DATE,
    values IN OUT NOCOPY numbers_varray,
    validity_flags IN OUT NOCOPY validity_rectype
    );
```

Remember that NOCOPY is a hint, not a command. This means that the compiler might silently decide it can't fulfill your request for a NOCOPY parameter treatment. See my book, *Oracle PL/SQL Programming: Guide to Oracle8i Features,* for more details.

To globalize a data structure, you want to create (if not already present) a package that can define and hold this persistent data structure. The "Resources" section offers an example script that allows you to compare the two approaches. Here, however, is the package specification, showing two versions of the same program (passtab)—one that accepts the collection as an argument, another that references it directly:b

```
CREATE OR REPLACE PACKAGE pkgvar
IS
    TYPE reward_rt IS RECORD (
        nm VARCHAR2(2000),
        comm NUMBER);

    TYPE reward_tt IS TABLE OF reward_rt
        INDEX BY BINARY_INTEGER;

    globtab reward_tt;

    PROCEDURE passtab (parmtab IN OUT reward_tt);
    PROCEDURE passtab;
END;
/
```

### Benefits

You can improve the performance of your application. You should consider either alternative, however, only after you have identified a clear performance problem in specific programs.

### Challenges

If you use NOCOPY or globalized data structures, the PL/SQL runtime engine no longer "roll back" changes when an exception occurs in your program. You can, as a consequence, end up with a data structure that is only partially updated.

### Resources

*pkgvar.pkg* and *pkgvar.tst*: A package and test script to both demonstrate the globalization technique and test its performance impact.

*nocopy.tst, nocopy2.tst,* and *nocopy3.tst*: Examples of scripts that examine the impact of the NOCOPY statement.

# Functions

Functions are program units that return a value through the RETURN clause of the program header.

## MOD-07: Limit functions to a single RETURN statement in the execution section.

A good general rule to follow as you write your PL/SQL programs is: "one way in and one way out." In other words, there should be just one way to enter or call a program (there is; you don't have any choice in this matter). And there should be one way out, one exit path from a program (or loop) on successful termination. By following this rule, you end up with code that is much easier to trace, debug, and maintain.

For a function, this means you should think of the executable section as a funnel; all the lines of code narrow down to the last executable statement:

```
RETURN return value;
```

Note the following:

- You can, and should, still have RETURN statements in your exception handlers. Not every exception should be passed unhandled from your function. See **EXC-07** for more information.
- It's possible (i.e., acceptable syntax) to use an "unqualified" RETURN statement in a procedure, as follows:

```
IF all_done
THEN
    RETURN;
END IF;
```

and the procedure immediately terminates and returns control. You shouldn't do this, however, as it results in unstructured code that's hard to debug and maintain This same recommendation holds for the initialization section of a package.

### Example

Here's a simple function that relies on multiple RETURNs:

```
CREATE OR REPLACE FUNCTION status_desc (
    cd_in IN VARCHAR2
)
    RETURN VARCHAR2
IS
BEGIN
```

```
    IF cd_in = 'C'
    THEN
        RETURN 'CLOSED';
    ELSIF cd_in = 'O'
    THEN
        RETURN 'OPEN';
    ELSIF cd_in = 'I'
    THEN
        RETURN 'INACTIVE';
    END IF;
END;
```

At first glance, this function looks very reasonable. Yet this function has a deep flaw, due to the reliance on separate RETURNs: if you don't pass in "C", "O", or "I" for the cd_in argument, the function raises:

```
ORA-06503: PL/SQL: Function returned without value
```

Here's a rewrite that relies on (a) a standard types package that avoids hard-coding a VARCHAR2 variable length (see **DAT-13**) and also gives names to literal values, and (b) a single RETURN at the end of the function:

```
CREATE OR REPLACE FUNCTION status_desc (
    cd_in IN VARCHAR2
)
    RETURN stdtypes.description_t
IS
    retval stdtypes.description_t;
BEGIN
    IF cd_in = stdtypes.c_closed_abbrev THEN
        retval := stdtypes.c_closed;
    ELSIF cd_in = stdtypes.c_open_abbrev THEN
        retval := stdtypes.c_open;
    ELSIF cd_in = stdtypes.c_inactive_abbrev ' THEN
        retval := stdtypes.c_inactive;
    END IF;
    RETURN retval;
END;
```

This program also safely and correctly returns NULL if the program doesn't receive a value of "C", "O", or "I", unlike the first implementation.

### Benefits

You're less likely to write a function that raises the exception "ORA-06503: PL/SQL: Function returned without value"—a nasty and embarrassing error.

A single RETURN function is easier to trace and debug, since you don't have to worry about multiple exit pathways from the function.

### Resources

*genmods.pkg*: A simple prototype of a function generator.

## MOD-08: Keep functions pure by avoiding [IN] OUT parameters.

The whole point of a function is to return a value (whether it's a single, scalar value or a composite, such as a record or a collection). If you also return data back through the parameter list with OUT or IN OUT arguments, the purpose and usage of the function is obscured. Oracle also places restrictions on how you can use functions that have OUT and IN OUT parameters—namely, you can't call that function from within a SQL statement.

If you need to return multiple pieces of information, take one of the following approaches:

*Return a record or collection of values*
 Make sure to publish the structure of your record or collection (the TYPE statement) in a package specification so that developers can understand and use the function more easily. Note that you can't call this function in a SQL statement if it returns a record or index-by table.

*Break up the single function into multiple functions, all returning scalar values*
 With this approach, you can call the functions from within SQL statements.

*Change your function into a procedure*
 Unless you need to call a function to return this information, just change it to a procedure returning multiple pieces of information.

### Example

Here's a function that returns several pieces of information about a book:

```
FUNCTION book_info (
    isbn_in IN book.isbn%TYPE,
    author_out OUT book.author%TYPE,
    page_count_out OUT book.page_count%TYPE)
    RETURN book.title%TYPE;
```

And now I use this function:

```
    l_title book.title%TYPE;
BEGIN
    l_title :=
        book_info (l_isbn, l_author, l_page_count);
```

Very confusing! The function seems to return a title, but what else does it do? It's hard to tell what is happening with the other parameters.

If, on the other hand, I restructure the function to return a record:

```
FUNCTION book_info (
    isbn_in IN book.isbn%TYPE)
    RETURN book%ROWTYPE;
```

the intent of the resulting code is more clear:

```
    one_book_rec book%ROWTYPE;
BEGIN
    one_book_rec := book_info (l_isbn);
```

### Benefits

Your functions are more likely to be used and reused, because they are defined in ways that make them easy to understand and apply in your own code.

Your function may then be callable from within a SQL statement, which encourages even wider use of this program. A function with an OUT argument can never be called from within SQL, Please note, though, that there are other restrictions on function calls from SQL. You may not, for example, call a function that returns a record (as shown in the preceding example).

### Challenges

You may need (or feel the need) to pass back status information as well as the data returned by the function. This comes up when calling PL/SQL code from non-Oracle languages such as Visual Basic. In this case, consider using a procedure instead of a function.

## MOD-09: Never return NULL from Boolean functions.

A Boolean function should return only TRUE or FALSE. If a Boolean function returns a NULL, how should the user of that function interpret and respond to that value? Does it indicate you passed in invalid data? Should it be considered TRUE or FALSE? Or should the developer test explicitly for NULL? Well, we should do explicit tests for NULL if we are uncertain about the function's behavior, but we rarely remember to do so or feel it's necessary to make the effort. Instead, we check for TRUE or FALSE and thus allow bugs to creep into our code.

If the Boolean function can return NULL, you probably need to look at the implementation of the function to determine the action to take on a NULL return value. Yet you will not always be able to (or want to) look at the function's body.

A non-Boolean function can use a NULL return value to indicate failure. A function that returns the title of a book for an ISBN number returns NULL for an invalid ISBN. That makes sense. On the other hand, a function that tells you whether or not a book is in print doesn't help you much if it returns NULL.

### Example

Here's a function that determines if a string is a valid ISBN number (it's not foolproof, but it gets across the basic idea):

```
CREATE OR REPLACE FUNCTION is_valid_isbn (
    isbn_in IN VARCHAR2)
    RETURN BOOLEAN
-- Ten digits separated by 4 hyphens
IS
    l_isbn book.isbn%TYPE;
BEGIN
    l_isbn := TRANSLATE (isbn_in,  'A-',  'A'); -- strip hyphens
    RETURN (LENGTH (l_isbn) = 10
            AND l_isbn + 0 = l_isbn);
                -- adding zero tests for numeric
EXCEPTION
    WHEN OTHERS THEN RETURN FALSE;
```

```
END is_valid_isbn;
/
```

And it works pretty well:

```
SQL> exec bpl (is_valid_isbn ('1-2-3-4'))
FALSE
SQL> exec bpl (is_valid_isbn ('1-12345-123-5'))
TRUE
```

But it returns NULL if an "empty" string is passed to it, which means that any use of is_valid_isbn should be combined with the NVL function, as in:

```
IF NVL (is_valid_isbn (1_isbn), FALSE)
```

The need to rely on NVL reduces the usefulness of the function. It should be rewritten to guarantee only one of two values returned: TRUE or FALSE. You will find such a rewrite in the file listed in the "Resources" section.

### Benefits

Developers are more likely to use your function within their application code.

### Resources

*isvalidisbn.fun*: This file contains the two implementations described in the example

# Triggers

Database triggers are a crucial part of any well-designed application. By placing logic in a trigger, you associate business rules closely with the database object, guaranteeing that these rules are always applied to any action taken against the object.

---

## MOD-10: Minimize the size of trigger execution sections.

Limit the number of lines of code in a trigger—even to the point of moving code into procedures, functions, or packages and calling them from the trigger.

Prior to Oracle7 Release 7.3, trigger code wasn't even stored in the database in compiled form. Each time a trigger was executed, it would also have to be compiled. Under these conditions, it was absolutely critical to move as much trigger code as possible to stored, precompiled procedures in order to improve the trigger's execution time.

Now, triggers are compiled just as procedures and functions are. Still, you should move as much of your business logic as possible to packaged programs.

### Example

Well, I could offer an example of pages and pages of code that are replaced by a single procedure call. That would certainly drive the point home—but at the expense of a few more trees. So instead, here is a very small trigger, but one that still exposes a business rule that should be hidden:

```
CREATE OR REPLACE TRIGGER check_employee_age
BEFORE INSERT OR UPDATE ON employee
BEGIN
    IF ADD_MONTHS (SYSDATE, -216) < :NEW.hire_date
    THEN
        RAISE_APPLICATION_ERROR (-20706,
            'Employee must be 18 to work here!');
    END IF;
END;
```

A much improved implementation would be:

```
CREATE OR REPLACE TRIGGER check_employee_age
BEFORE INSERT OR UPDATE ON employee
BEGIN
    IF employee_rules.emp_too_young (:NEW.hire_date)
    THEN
        err_pkg.rase (employee_rules.c_errnum_emp_too_young,
            :NEW.employee_id);
    END IF;
END;
```

Now that business rule (which in the "real world" might have been very complex and taken up several lines of code) is moved to the package. I have also avoided the hard-coding of a RAISE_APPLICATION_ERROR call relying on my standard error package (see **EXC-04**).

### Benefits

Keeping trigger code small provides a modular code layout that's easy to maintain and debug.

You greatly reduce the chance of introducing redundant business rule logic into your application if you always insist on moving such logic to packages.

### Challenges

Within a row-level trigger, you can reference the old and new values of the row's columns with the :NEW and :OLD pseudo-records. You can't, however, pass these structures as parameters, nor can you reference them in dynamic SQL code. These restrictions often force you to write more—and very cumbersome—logic than desired in the trigger. See the "Resources" section for a program you can use to generate code that will at least save you some time in dealing with :OLD and :NEW.

### Resources

*genmods.pkg*: The genmods.use_new and genmods.use_old procedures within this package generate procedure calls that "explode" the pseudo-records into individual arguments (one per column) that can be passed to stored programs. Here's an example session:

```
SQL> exec genmods.use_new ('employee', 'myprog')
myprog (
    :NEW.EMPLOYEE_ID,
```

```
    :NEW.LAST_NAME,
    :NEW.FIRST_NAME,
    :NEW.MIDDLE_INITIAL,
    :NEW.JOB_ID,
    :NEW.MANAGER_ID,
    :NEW.HIRE_DATE,
    :NEW.SALARY,
    :NEW.COMMISSION,
    :NEW.DEPARTMENT_ID,
    :NEW.EMPNO,
    :NEW.ENAME,
    :NEW.CREATED_BY,
    :NEW.CREATED_ON,
    :NEW.CHANGED_BY,
    :NEW.CHANGED_ON
);
```

## MOD-11: Consolidate "overlapping" DML triggers to control execution order.

While it's possible to create many DML triggers of the same type on a table, it isn't possible to guarantee the order in which they fire. While several theories abound about firing order (including reverse order of creation or object ID), it isn't advisable to rely on theories when designing database triggers. Instead, you should consolidate into a single trigger all triggers that fire under the same conditions.

### Example

When inserting a value of 1 for the following ID field, what value will wind up in the table?

```
CREATE OR REPLACE TRIGGER increment_by_one
BEFORE INSERT ON id_table
FOR EACH ROW
BEGIN
  :new.id := :new.id + 1;
END;
/

CREATE OR REPLACE TRIGGER increment_by_two
BEFORE INSERT ON id_table
FOR EACH ROW
BEGIN
  IF :new.id > 1 THEN
    :new.id := :new.id + 2;
  END IF;
END;
/
```

The answer is, in reality, indeterminate; you can't accurately predict the behavior of such a system of triggers.

### Benefits

You don't have to be concerned about the order in which triggers fire when the application is rebuilt, moved, or upgraded.

### Challenges

It may be difficult to move complex code into a single trigger.

You may also have some trouble identifying triggers that fire under the same conditions. See the "Resources" section for a query you can run that should help answer this question.

### Resources

*multiple_triggers.sql*: Contains a detailed working version of the example.

*trigger_conflict.sql*: A simple query against the USR_TRIGGERS data dictionary view that helps you identify potentially conflicting triggers.

## MOD-12: Raise exceptions to report on do-nothing INSTEAD OF triggers.

If you execute an UPDATE statement and it doesn't identify any rows to update, Oracle doesn't raise an error. In many cases, that is fine. In other cases, it might indicate an error. The situation is the same with INSTEAD OF triggers. These triggers allow you to specify an alternative operation that will take place instead of the normal DML action with which the trigger is associated.

If the INSTEAD OF trigger doesn't execute any DML at all but doesn't raise an exception, it doesn't report any error back to the calling program. While in some cases this may be the desired behavior, you usually want to raise an exception, and perhaps also log the fact that a failure occurred

### Example

Consider the following rather selfish trigger. I have created a view called best_sellers that sits on top of the book table. When you insert a row into best_sellers, it actually inserts a row only if the publisher of the book is O'Reilly & Associates!

```
CREATE OR REPLACE TRIGGER instead_of_best_sellers
   INSTEAD OF INSERT
   ON best_sellers
BEGIN
   IF :new.publisher = 'O''REILLY & ASSOCIATES'
   THEN
      INSERT INTO book (
         author, title, isbn, publisher)
      VALUES (
         :new.author, :new.title, :new.isbn, :new.publisher);
   END IF;
END;
```

That's an unethical thing to do, but with the way the trigger is written, there's no immediate notification that a best seller by, say, Oracle Press, wasn't added to the table. Here's a more principled and appropriate way to write this code:

```
CREATE OR REPLACE TRIGGER instead_of_best_sellers
   INSTEAD OF INSERT
   ON best_sellers
BEGIN
   IF :new.publisher = 'O''REILLY & ASSOCIATES'
   THEN
      INSERT INTO book (
         author, title, isbn, publisher)
      VALUES (
         :new.author, :new.title, :new.isbn, :new.publisher);
   ELSE
      err_pkg.raise (book_rules.c_errnum_only_oreilly);
   END IF;
END;
```

Now, at least the user is notified of the acceptable types of books for best sellers!

### Benefits

Phantom DML operations are diagnosed and reported; you aren't left to wonder what actually happened when the trigger fired.

You get back a positive indication that the DML failed, just as you do in the case of failed DML on a table.

### Resources

*instead_of_nothing.sql*: Contains a complete example of handling the situation versus not handling the situation.

---

## MOD-13: Implement server problem logs and "to do" lists using database triggers.

Oracle8*i* now offers database-level triggers that can be fired on events such as LOGON, LOGOFF, and SERVERERROR. These triggers offer all sorts of new possibilities for a DBA but can sometimes lead to problems.

Suppose, for instance, that an application encounters the ORA-01659 error ("unable to allocate next extent"). The solution is to add a data file to the applicable tablespace. With a SERVERERROR trigger, you can actually trap this problem and, right on the spot, add a data file. That's all well and good, but while the data file is being added (which can take quite a while), the user process is blocked. Imagine a poor end user sitting at his terminal staring at a blank screen for 10 minutes while the database adds a dataflow to fix an error he wasn't even aware had occurred.

A far superior approach to take is to first, adopt as a guiding principle that whenever possible the user process is allowed to continue uninterrupted. The SERVERERROR trigger should then simply logs an error or, even better, sends a message to a DBA (via the Oracle Advanced Queuing facility, for example) or builds a to-do list. This list can then be parsed and processed by a background database job run at regular intervals.

Database-level triggers fire as autonomous transactions, making it far easier to place an entry into a "to do" table, without affecting the user transaction.

### Example

Here's a simple SERVERERROR trigger that adds an item to the DBA to-do list:

```
CREATE OR REPLACE TRIGGER db_error_handler
AFTER SERVERERROR ON DATABASE
BEGIN
  IF ORA_IS_SERVERERROR (-1659) THEN
    db_to_do_list.add_item('ADD_DATAFILE');
  END IF;
END;
```

### Benefits

Processes that encounter errors don't have to wait for the complete fix.

This is a good way to build in logging that helps identify database or application problems at a low level of database operations.

### Challenges

You must ensure that the "to-do" list is processed in a timely manner while not overwhelming database resources.

Sometimes, the information required to fix an error isn't obvious or available within the confines of the trigger. In the preceding example, the name of the tablespace requiring a data file isn't readily available. You can, however, obtain the table name from ora_dict_obj_name (see **MOD-14**), and from that derive the tablespace name.

## MOD-14: Use ORA_% public synonyms to reference database and schema event trigger attributes.

Within the confines of DDL and database event triggers, there is a lot of information available about what specifically caused the trigger to fire, for example, the exact table and column or the name of the user. This information is available via a set of PL/SQL functions contained in the DBMS_STANDARD package. Always reference these functions via the public synonyms (ORA_%) also provided (and defined in the *dbmstrig.sql* file in the *Rdbms/Admin* subdirectory of installed Oracle software).

Here's a small subset of the functions available (consult *dbmstrig.sql* for a complete list):

* ora_sysevent: The system event that invokes the system trigger
* ora_dict_obj_owner: The object owner on which the DDL statement is being done
* ora_dict_obj_name: The object name on which the DDL statement is being performed

### Example

```
CREATE OR REPLACE TRIGGER after_create
AFTER CREATE ON SCHEMA
DECLARE
  /*
```

```
    || The BAD way. Direct calls to the functions in DBMS_STANDARD
    */
    v_type VARCHAR2(30) := DICTIONARY_OBJ_TYPE;
    v_name VARCHAR2(30) := DICTIONARY_OBJ_NAME;
BEGIN
    -- the GOOD way; via the synonyms
    INSERT INTO log_create
    VALUES(ORA_DICT_OBJ_TYPE,
           ORA_DICT_OBJ_NAME);
    -- the BAD way; via direct calls
    INSERT INTO log_create
    VALUES(v_type,
           v_name);
END;
```

### Benefits

Your code is protected from future changes.

### Resources

*always_use_ora.sql*: Contains the preceding example.

---

## MOD-15: Validate complex business rules with DML triggers.

Foreign key, NOT NULL, and check constraints provide mechanisms to validate simple business rules like:

An account transaction must be for a valid account.

or:

If the transaction type is DEP the amount must be entered.

However, there are some cases they simply can't handle. Consider the following requirements:

If the account transaction has been approved, it can't be updated.

Account transactions can't be created with approved status.

Regardless of the complexity of the logic behind evaluating the approved status of a transaction, it probably isn't something a simple constraint can handle. In these cases, database triggers step in with the ability to support arbitrarily complex logic, while simultaneously guaranteeing that applications can't sidestep the rules.

### Example

Here are some examples of simple trigger logic that still can't be handled with constraints.

If the account transaction has been approved, it can't be updated:

```
CREATE TRIGGER cannot_change_approved
BEFORE UPDATE ON account_transaction
FOR EACH ROW
BEGIN
    IF :OLD.approved_yn = constants.yes
    THEN
```

```
      err_pkg.raise (account_rules.c_no_change_after_approval);
   END IF;
END;
```

Account transactions can't be created with approved status:

```
CREATE TRIGGER cannot_create_approved
BEFORE INSERT ON account_transaction
FOR EACH ROW
BEGIN
  IF :NEW.approved_yn = 'Y'
  THEN
     err_pkg.raise (account_rules.c_no_preapproval);
  END IF;
END;
```

These business rules must be validated in triggers because the type of DML being performed must be recognized, and the developer needs access to old and new values. This information isn't available within NOT NULL, referential integrity, or check constraints.

### Benefits

Careful planning and design allow even the most complex business rules to be validated in DML triggers.

If business rules are checked with triggers, user interfaces aren't required to check them. This makes changes easier to implement.

---

## MOD-16: Populate columns of derived values with triggers.

Some applications require that extra information be stored in a record whenever it's inserted, updated, or deleted. This information may or may not be supplied by the application itself.

### Example

In this example, the date a record is updated is recorded within the record itself:

```
CREATE OR REPLACE TRIGGER set_updated_fields
BEFORE UPDATE ON account_transaction
FOR EACH ROW
BEGIN
  IF :NEW.updated_date IS NULL
  THEN
     :NEW.updated_date := SYSDATE;
  END IF;
END;
```

### Benefits

You can guarantee that the fields will be populated because all records are processed by the triggers.

### Challenges

If you have a set of standard columns whose values are set through triggers, those columns should not be provided values in application DML statements. It would probably make sense to build views on top of the base tables that hide the derived-value columns.

## MOD-17: Use operational directives to provide more meaningful error messages from within triggers.

You can create a single trigger that fires for more than one DML operation, as in:

```
CREATE OR REPLACE TRIGGER check_for_reserved_status
    BEFORE UPDATE OR INSERT ON book
FOR EACH ROW
```

This allows you to consolidate logic that must be applied to all these operations into a single program unit. If you do this, however, you should take advantage of built-in functions defined in the default DBMS_STANDARD package to help you determine exactly which type of operation was executed.

Here are the headers of those special functions or "operational directives":

```
FUNCTION INSERTING RETURN BOOLEAN;
FUNCTION DELETING  RETURN BOOLEAN;
FUNCTION UPDATING  RETURN BOOLEAN;
FUNCTION UPDATING (COLNAM VARCHAR2) RETURN BOOLEAN;
```

### Example

This example allows a single trigger to ensure that approved transactions are neither changed nor deleted, while displaying an informative message when they are:

```
CREATE OR REPLACE TRIGGER check_approved
    BEFORE UPDATE OR DELETE
    ON account_transaction
    FOR EACH ROW
BEGIN
    IF :old.approved_yn = 'Y'
    THEN
        IF updating
        THEN
            err_pkg.raise (
                te_account_transaction.c_no_update_after_approved);
        ELSE
            err_pkg.raise (
                te_account_transaction.c_no_delete_after_approved);
        END IF;
    END IF;
END;
```

### Benefits

Single triggers can provide meaningful messages.

# 8

# *Package Construction*

Packages are the fundamental building blocks of any well-designed application built in the Oracle PL/SQL language (at least until Oracle improves the robustness of its object implementation!). A package consists of up to two elements: the specification and the body. The specification tells a user what she can do with the package: what programs can be called, what data structures and user-defined types can be referenced, and so on. The package body implements any programs in the package specification; it can also contain private (i.e., not shown in the specification) data structures and program units.

## *PKG-01: Group related data structures and functionality together in a single package.*

Even if you don't take advantage of features unique to packages, such as persistent data, you can still use packages to organize—and store together—related code and data structures.

Without packages, you might end up with several hundred standalone procedures and functions and many repeated cursor, TYPE, and variable declarations.

A package gives a name to a set of program elements: procedures, functions, user-defined types, variable and constant declarations, cursors, and so on. By creating a package for each distinct area of functionality, you create intuitive containers for that functionality.

### *Example*

As I go about building a library management system, I quickly identify the following functional areas:

*Borrower information*
> Maintain underlying table, establish rules about who is a valid borrower.

*Book information*
> Maintain underlying table, define validation for ISBN, and so on.

*Borrowing history*
> Maintain underlying table that tracks who took out what and when.

*Overdue fines*
> Collection of all formulas and business rules for processing overdue charges.

*Special reservations*
> Maintain underlying table and collect all rules governing how a borrower can reserve a book.

*Publisher information*
> Maintain underlying table.

I can now create separate packages for each bunch of data or functional specification. For example, the overdue package would contain all programs related to calculating and displaying overdue fine information. If I need any TYPEs (collections and records, for example) to declare or manipulate overdue data, I would also define those in the overdue package.

### Benefits

It's much easier to build, find, and maintain programs when they are organized by logical area into separate packages.

Once you have segregated programs and data into their own packages, you can more easily leverage special features of packages (persistent data, initialization section, overloading) to improve performance and functionality.

### Resources

*te_employee.pks* and *te_employee.pkb*: Table encapsulation packages feature "high cohesion" (grouping together of related programs). Such packages offer a set of procedures and functions that allow a developer to manipulate the underlying data structure (table or view) without writing any explicit SQL.

*xfile.pkg*: The xfile class (built on top of the JFile Java class) offers "one stop shopping" for all file-related processing in a PL/SQL environment.

---

## PKG-02: Provide well-defined interfaces to business data and functional manipulation using packages.

Humans can handle only so much complexity at once. The details and nuances of any decent-sized application overwhelm the human mind. Use packages to hide—or at least attempt to organize—the mind-boggling complexity. Expose the underlying data and business rules in an orderly and manageable fashion through the package specification.

This technique is crucially important when implementing core business rules in your application. Every such rule should be hidden behind a function and defined in the appropriate package.

In addition, hide all the SQL for a given table or business entity behind a package interface (this process is called *table encapsulation*). Rather than write an INSERT statement in your program, call an insert procedure. See **SQL-15** for more details.

## Example

Let's look at a simple example: building a timing utility. The DBMS_UTILITY.GET_ TIME built-in function returns the number of hundredths of seconds that have elapsed since an arbitrary point in time. You call it twice and subtract the difference to calculate elapsed time (down to the hundredth of a second), as in:

```
DECLARE
    l_start PLS_INTEGER;
    l_end PLS_INTEGER;
BEGIN
    l_start := DBMS_UTILITY.GET_TIME;
    overdue.calculate_fines;
    l_end := DBMS_UTILITY.GET_TIME;
    pl ('Calculated fines in ' ||
        (l_end - l_start) / 100 || ' seconds');
END;
```

I have two concerns: (a) that's a lot of code to write to simply calculate elapsed time, and (b) the formula is exposed that calculates elapsed time. What if the formula changes? Ah, you're probably asking: How could a formula this simple change? Well, it turns out that this formula can sometimes result in a *negative* elapsed time, because DBMS_UTILITY.GET_TIME occasionally "rolls over" to zero.

So rather than writing code like that shown in the preceding example, you are much better served by building a simple package as follows:

```
CREATE OR REPLACE PACKAGE tmr
IS
    PROCEDURE capture;
    PROCEDURE show_elapsed;
END tmr;
/
CREATE OR REPLACE PACKAGE BODY tmr
IS
    c_bignum INTEGER := POWER(2,32);
    last_timing NUMBER := NULL;

    PROCEDURE capture IS
    BEGIN
      last_timing := DBMS_UTILITY.GET_TIME;
    END capture;

    PROCEDURE show_elapsed IS
    BEGIN
       pl (MOD (DBMS_UTILITY.GET_TIME -
                  last_timing + c_bignum, c_bignum));
    END show_elapsed;
END tmr;
/
```

This package-based implementation now allows you to calculate elapsed time as follows:

```
BEGIN
    tmr.capture;
    overdue.calculate_fines;
    tmr.show_elapsed;
END;
```

### Benefits

By using packages to hide complexity, you naturally employ stepwise refinement (a.k.a. top-down design). The resulting code is easier to understand, use, and maintain.

By hiding formulas, you can fix them and enhance them as needed over time.

### Resources

*tmr.pkg*: The simplest version of the timer package

*PLVtmr.pkg*: A more complete implementation

*tmr81.ot*: An object-based timer

---

## PKG-03: Freeze and build package specifications before implementing package bodies.

Develop a "specifications first" discipline: put off writing package bodies as long as possible. Instead, sit back, relax, and brainstorm about the kinds of things you want to do with each package (based, of course, on requirements provided by the users). Write out those things-to-do as procedure and function headers in the specification. Do this for a whole bunch of packages you need to build.

Then try them out. Even if you don't built the package bodies, you can still write programs based on the headers. By doing this, you often uncover errors in the requirements, missing parameters, and so on. Since you haven't yet written the implementations, it's easy to clarify what the user wants and modify the package specifications.

Once you are confident that the specifications reflect the application needs, dive into those package bodies!

### Example

We are building a telesales call management system. Management just told us that due to the upcoming IPO, we have to get everything done in two months. Yikes! My first inclination is to start writing code madly, but the DBAs haven't finished designing the tables, and the users are still thrashing. I can't wait, though, so I take what requirements have been set and brainstorm via package specifications.

I know that I have to do some analysis, so I quickly put together this specification:

```
CREATE OR REPLACE PACKAGE analysis
IS
    FUNCTION avg_workload (
        dept_id IN INTEGER) RETURN NUMBER;
```

```
      FUNCTION workload (
          operator_id IN INTEGER) RETURN NUMBER;
      FUNCTION avg_numcalls (
          dept_id IN INTEGER) RETURN NUMBER;
   END analysis;
```

I don't yet know *how* to calculate the average workload for a department, but I know I will need it. I also need to perform some call maintenance, and according to the documentation, I need to transfer a call to a new department:

```
CREATE OR REPLACE PACKAGE callmaint
IS
   PROCEDURE transfer (
       call_id IN INTEGER, dept_id IN INTEGER;
   END callmaint;
```

Now, I can perform two pieces of "magic":

• I can compile both specifications, since they don't rely on any %TYPE declarations to tables that don't exist. That way, I can make sure their syntax is valid.

• I can write other programs that use these programs, such as the load-balancing "assign a call" procedure, shown here:

```
CREATE OR REPLACE PROCEDURE assign_call
    (call_in IN INTEGER,
     oper_in IN INTEGER,
     dept_in IN INTEGER)
IS
BEGIN
   IF analysis.workload (oper_in) <
          analysis.avg_workload (dept_in)
   THEN
       callmaint.transfer (call_in, dept_in);
   END IF;
END assign_call;
```

Once again, I can verify that this code compiles (though I can't run it). I can also walk through this very readable code and check for logical errors. Allow me to read it to you:

> If the workload for this operator is less than the average workload of the department, then transfer the call to that department.

Wait a minute, that doesn't sound right. Shouldn't I transfer the call to that operator who is underutilized? So I check with the users, get confirmation of their mistake, and in minutes have corrected the callmaint specification and the assign_call procedure. No need to fix the package body, though, since I held off implementing it.

### Benefits

By concentrating on the way that different programs interact with each other, the resulting software is better behaved and more easily changed over time.

You spend less time fixing errors later in the development cycle, since you can more easily identify problems before extensive coding has even begun.

### Challenges

You might get nervous because you are holding off writing the "real" code, the package body, while the clock ticks away. The time spent on this upfront design verification will, however, save you hours of fixes and debugging later on. You can also create the package body that contains "stub" subprograms, in which each procedure or function contains the minimum amount of code needed to get the package body to compile. The code can be run but, of course, it won't actually do anything (except perhaps allow you to trace execution and validate overall logical flow).

## PKG-04: Implement flexible, user-adjustable functionality using package state toggles and related techniques.

As you rely more and more on packages to offer functionality to programmers on your team or in your company, you want to design those packages to be flexible and responsive to varying user needs.

You certainly don't want programmers going into the package bodies and changing implementations. You also don't want them making copies of your code and then producing their own variations.

Instead, add programs to the package specification that allow developers to modify (within certain accepted pathways) the behavior of your package to fit their varying requirements. These programs might turn on/off certain features ("toggles") or might set internal package values.

The most important feature of these programs is that they allow the package to change its behavior without having to change the source code.

### Example

I have decided to build a check-out package that allows librarians to check books out of their collection. The default rule is that a person can have a maximum of 10 books checked out at any time. I can write my package to hard-code that rule as follows:

```
CREATE OR REPLACE PACKAGE BODY checkout_pkg
IS
    c_max_allowed CONSTANT PLS_INTEGER := 10;

    FUNCTION can_check_out (
        borrower_id IN borrower.id%TYPE,
        isbn_in IN book.isn%TYPE)
        RETURN BOOLEAN
    IS
        l_checked_out PLS_INTEGER;
        l_book_is_available BOOLEAN;
    BEGIN
        l_checked_out :=
            checked_out_count (borrower_id);
        l_book_is_available :=
            book_available (isbn_id);
        RETURN (l_checked_out < c_max_allowed
```

```
                          AND l_book_is_available);
        END can_check_out;
           ...
```

But this approach doesn't let a librarian override this rule, which he might need to do with a professional researcher, for example. A much better approach is to offer, in the specification, a way to change the checkout limits, within reasonable boundaries. Here's a modified package specification:

```
CREATE OR REPLACE PACKAGE BODY checkout_pkg
IS
    PROCEDURE set_checkout_limit (count_in IN PLS_INTEGER);
    FUNCTION checkout_limit RETURN PLS_INTEGER;

    FUNCTION can_check_out (
        borrower_id IN borrower.id%TYPE,
        isbn_in IN book.isn%TYPE)
        RETURN BOOLEAN;
```

The implementation of this override is simple: change the constant to a variable and modify it from within set_checkout_limit:

```
CREATE OR REPLACE PACKAGE BODY checkout_pkg
IS
    g_max_allowed PLS_INTEGER := 10;

    PROCEDURE set_checkout_limit (
        count_in IN PLS_INTEGER) IS
    BEGIN
        g_max_allowed :=
            LEAST (GREATEST (count_in, 1), 20);
    END set_checkout_limit;

    FUNCTION checkout_limit RETURN PLS_INTEGER IS
    BEGIN
        RETURN g_max_allowed;
    END checkout_limit;
```

Another example of this technique is the on/off switch you build to implement a "window" in a package (see **PKG-05**).

## Benefits

The increased flexibility makes it more likely that the package is used and reused. Code reuse generally improves the quality of your application and reduces the resources needed to test and maintain the code base.

You can often layer toggles and other setting programs on top of an existing package; it doesn't all have to be figured out in advance.

## Challenges

From a design standpoint, you can implement this flexibility either as a package-level setting or by adding another parameter to your programs. Choose the package-level approach if the setting or switch is a preference the user will want to apply to the overall package behavior, and not just a single program. You can even build a small GUI applet that allows a developer to easily change these settings.

### Resources

*watch.pkg*: This package, used to trace program execution, offers the ability to switch output between the screen and database pipes.

---

## PKG-05: Build trace "windows" into your packages using standardized programs.

On the one hand, it's very helpful to use packages to hide complexity. On the other hand, it's often the case that users can be greatly aided by being able to look inside packages and watch what's happening.

You can easily build a "read-only" window into a package. Users can open the window when and if he wants to, watch what the package is doing (or at least what the author of the package claims the package is doing), and then shut the window when that information isn't needed.

To build a window, you will need to:

- Add tracing code inside the package body.
- Supply an on-off switch in the specification so that users can open and close the window.

### Example

My overdue fines package allows a user to set the daily fine rate, as shown by this partial package body:

```
CREATE OR REPLACE PACKAGE BODY overdue_pkg
IS
    g_daily_fine NUMBER := .10;

    PROCEDURE set_daily_fine (fine_in IN NUMBER) IS
    BEGIN
        g_daily_fine :=
            GREATEST (LEAST (fine_in, .25), .05);
    END set_daily_fine;
    ...
```

I now want to add a trace to this package so that a user of *overdue_pkg* can see what the daily fine is being set to when her application runs. First, I add an on-off switch to the package specification and body:

```
CREATE OR REPLACE PACKAGE overdue_pkg
IS
    ... other elements in package

    PROCEDURE trc;
    PROCEDURE notrc;
    FUNCTION tracing RETURN BOOLEAN;
END overdue_pkg;
```

Then, I add my trace to the *set_daily_fine* procedure:

```
PROCEDURE set_daily_fine (fine_in IN NUMBER)
IS
BEGIN
   IF tracing
   THEN
      watch.action ('set_daily_fine', fine_in);
   END IF;

   g_daily_fine :=
      GREATEST (LEAST (fine_in, .25), .05);
END set_daily_fine;
```

Rather than call DBMS_OUTPUT.PUT_LINE or even my enhanced pl procedure, notice that I call watch.action. The watch package is a more robust tracing mechanism. Among other features, it allows you to direct output to a database pipe, bypassing the buffer limitations of DBMS_OUTPUT.

Now, when I want to watch what is happening inside my overdue package, I simply turn on trace for my session before I run my application code:

```
SQL> exec overdue_pkg.trc
SQL> exec library_test
```

### Benefits

This "read-only" window into a package can help you ensure that you're using the package properly or allow you to confirm that the data you're passing into the package is correct. Such windows increase your confidence in the package and allow you to use it more effectively. The on-off switch for the window is based on the "get and set" technique discussed in **DAT-15**.

Windows are easy to add to your package after you have written the base code. Just add an on-off switch and put an IF statement inside the appropriate module.

### Challenges

If you add trace calls, add them comprehensively, taking into account the perspective and needs of the user. Looking through a smoky window may be more confusing than not being able to see at all.

It's worth coming up with a plan for where and when you will insert trace calls in your code. Take into account possible impact on performance and readability. You may also find yourself adding trace logic iteratively as you work on different sections of code, in order to watch several computations or logic paths.

### Resources

*overdue.pkg*: The overdue package

*watch.pkg*: A watch package used to perform tracing

## A Robust Tracing Mechanism

When watching values inside a loop, many values may be generated (hundreds of thousands if you loop that many times). Conditional logic can be used to only display values when specific criteria are met. For example, while processing tens of thousands of claims, we wanted to trace only specific claims. So I built a package that allowed us to store those claim numbers in a packaged index-by table (before we actually ran the claims processing program). If any of those claims came up, the trace mechanism was enabled only for those claims. A global debug flag turned debugging on or off in general, and a local flag turned it on or off for just those claims pre-populated in the index-by table (but only if the global debug flag was turned on). A function provided the interface to the index-by table.

—Dan Clamage

## PKG-06: Use package body persistent data structures to cache and optimize data-driven processing.

When you declare data inside a package but not within any individual procedure or function in the package, that data persists for your entire session.* A package-level collection, for example, retains its values (say, 1000 rows of data) until you DELETE one or more rows from the collection, close your connection, or recompile the package.

This data persistence means you can use package data as a "local" cache—local to that single session/user. The System Global Area (SGA) acts as a cache for all users and greatly improves overall. database performance. Your own session-specific cache can improve your application performance. You can cache at multiple levels:

- A single value, such as the name of the current user
- A record of values, such as the default configuration for the current user
- An entire collection or list of values, such as the result set of a query that must be processed multiple times

Regardless of the complexity of data, the conditions and steps for caching are similar:

- The data must be static for the duration of the session. It's possible to come up with ways to update the cache, but such efforts are likely to cancel out performance gains.
- You need to declare the data structures inside the package body so that you can manage their contents and integrity (see **DAT-15**).

---

* You can insert the PRAGMA SERIALLY_REUSABLE statement into your package if you don't want package level data to be persistent.

- You also need to build access programs to those data structures so that even inside the package body, you manipulate the cache through a well-defined interface.

## *Example*

For reasons of space, I will show the simplest package-based caching mechanism here. See the "Resources" section for more complex sample packages.

Consider the USER function. It returns the name of the currently connected user. This value never changes during your session, right? The USER function in PL/SQL is implemented as follows (as defined in the STANDARD package, and with less-than-ideal formatting):

```
function USER return varchar2 is
c varchar2(255);
begin
    select user into c from sys.dual;
    return c;
end;
```

So every time you call USER in PL/SQL, it runs a query. That is quite unnecessary, and you can use caching to ensure that this query is run just once per session:

```
CREATE OR REPLACE PACKAGE thisuser
IS
    name CONSTANT VARCHAR2(30) := USER;
END thisuser;
/
```

Now you can reference the value of USER without multiple calls to USER, like this:

```
FOR user_rec IN user_cur
LOOP
    IF user_rec.user_name = thisuser.name
    THEN
        . . .
```

See the "Resources" section for a reference to the thisuser package; there you will find a script you can run to test the performance advantage of thisuser over direct, repetitive calls to USER.

## *Benefits*

This technique improves application performance by avoiding unnecessary and (relatively speaking) slow data access through the SGA.

It's especially handy when you execute long-running batch processes that must perform multiple passes through large result sets. Load up the query results in a collection of records, and then you have bidirectional, random access to the data for your batch process.

## *Challenges*

Each session has its own copy of package data, and Oracle uses real memory for this session data. So if you plan to cache data, be aware of the volume of data and the number of users who will cache it.

---

## Put USER in a Package Variable

We used the USER function to differentiate report data being generated by each user, so two people could run the same report with different criteria and not stomp on each other. We used function USER everywhere—in hundreds of packages. Then one day, when the DBA was figuring out how to migrate our current platform to AIX, he realized that the USER value would have to be replaced with *v$session.osuser*, for network-related reasons. We had to go back and fix a lot of packages. If only we had stored the USER value in a package variable, we would just have needed to change it in one place.

—Dan Clamage

---

### Resources

*init.pkg* and *init.tst*: An example package and script to compare the performance of caching a record of data.

*emplu.pkg* and *emplu.tst*: An example package and script to compare the performance of caching multiple rows of data.

---

## PKG-07: Insulate applications from Oracle version sensitivity using version-specific implementations.

Many organizations need to write code that will run on different Oracle versions (such as Oracle 7.3 and Oracle 8.1). There are two approaches you might follow in this situation:

- Use "lowest common denominator" features that are available in all versions.
- Use the best and most appropriate features available in each version.

If you take the first approach, you can maintain just one version of code, but you will also sacrifice significant functionality and performance advantages. If you take the second approach, you can avoid maintaining multiple copies of the code by (a) using packages to isolate those differences, and (b) relying on the separation of package specification and body to "execute around" compilation errors.

Here are the basic steps you need to take to achieve this effect:

1. Extract all version-specific logic into separate package bodies, separated by database version.
2. Create a function that returns the current Oracle version.
3. Modify or create the main (public) package to call each of the version-specific programs, based on the current Oracle version.
4. Compile and use the code in each different database version.

This last point is, in a way, the most interesting. You see, at least one of your package bodies will actually fail to compile—and you won't care! The package body for Oracle8*i*, for example, doesn't compile in Oracle 7.3. But that doesn't matter at all, because (a) the package specification compiles, and that's all the outer package needs for it to compile, and (b) the code in the body that didn't compile will never be called.

The following example demonstrates this in a simple and easy to understand way.

### Example

Suppose I need to build an error-logging package that will be used in Oracle 7.3 and Oracle8*i* (8.1). In Oracle8*i*, I want to take advantage of autonomous transactions, allowing the log entry to be immediately saved to the database without affecting the main transaction. First, I create the specifications for my generic logging package and a separate package for my Oracle8*i*-specific code:

```
CREATE OR REPLACE PACKAGE log_pkg
IS
    PROCEDURE putline (
        code_in IN INTEGER, text_in IN VARCHAR2);
END log_pkg;
/

CREATE OR REPLACE PACKAGE log81_pkg
IS
    PROCEDURE putline (
        code_in IN INTEGER, text_in IN VARCHAR2);
END log81_pkg;
/
```

My logging package body determines the Oracle version with a query against the PRODUCT_COMPONENT_VERSION data dictionary view and stores it in a global package variable:

```
CREATE OR REPLACE PACKAGE BODY log_pkg
IS
    g_version VARCHAR2 (100);

    FUNCTION oraversion RETURN VARCHAR2
    IS
        retval VARCHAR2 (100);
    BEGIN
        SELECT SUBSTR (version, 1, 3)
          INTO retval
          FROM product_component_version
         WHERE UPPER (product) LIKE 'ORACLE7%'
            OR UPPER (product) LIKE 'PERSONAL ORACLE%'
            OR UPPER (product) LIKE 'ORACLE8%';
        RETURN retval;
    END oraversion;
```

I then implement the putline procedure using conditional logic either to call the Oracle8*i* logging program or to do the "normal" INSERT (the best I can do in Oracle7 and Oracle8):

```
    PROCEDURE putline (
        code_in IN INTEGER, text_in IN VARCHAR2)
    IS
    BEGIN
```

```
        IF g_version = '8.1'
        THEN
           log81_pkg.putline (code_in, text_in);
        ELSE
           INSERT INTO logtab
              VALUES (code_in, text_in, SYSDATE, USER);
        END IF;
     END putline;
BEGIN
    -- Populate the version in the init. section.
    g_version := oraversion;
END log_pkg;
/
```

This package body compiles because the log81_pkg specification has already been defined; the package body isn't needed to get this far. Now let's try the package body for Oracle8*i* processing:

```
CREATE OR REPLACE PACKAGE BODY log81_pkg
IS
    PROCEDURE putline (
       code_in IN INTEGER, text_in IN VARCHAR2)
    IS
       PRAGMA AUTONOMOUS_TRANSACTION;
    BEGIN
       INSERT INTO logtab
          VALUES (code_in, text_in, SYSDATE, USER);
       COMMIT;
    EXCEPTION
       WHEN OTHERS
       THEN
           ROLLBACK;
    END putline;
END log81_pkg;
/
```

This package body doesn't compile in an Oracle7 environment, but the log_pkg.put_line procedure still works because log81_pkg.put_line is never called. The log.tst script demonstrates this behavior. For those of us running Oracle8i, the second half of the script "mimics" an Oracle7 environment by hard-coding the version and causing compile errors in the log81_pkg body.

---

You might also consider using the DBMS_SQL package (available in all current and future versions of the Oracle RDBMS) to execute a PL/SQL block that's constructed at runtime. The package compiles because the compiler is ignorant of version-specific dependencies hidden in the text string.

---

### Benefits

You can build and maintain one version of your code that works across multiple versions of the Oracle database.

### Challenges

Make sure that the function retrieving the Oracle database version works on your instance (I have confirmed the logic for Oracle7, Oracle8, and Oracle8*i* through 8.1.6).

You will sometimes want to use version-specific features in the package specification, such as Oracle8*i*'s NOCOPY parameter hint, the DETERMINISTIC pragma, and the AUTHID clause. This technique will then not work.

### Resources

*log.pkg* and *log.tst*: The log package and test script that demonstrate the techniques you need for this best practice.

---

## PKG-08: Avoid bloating package code with unnecessary but easy-to-build modules.

This best practice definitely applies to the author of this book. Once you get started building packages, especially packages that provide an interface to underlying functionality, it's so, so easy to get excited about all the possibilities, all the different programs that can and should be a part of that interface. Why not add a function that calculates X, or a procedure that displays Y?

The result can be best characterized by a rephrasing of that oft-repeated riddle:

If you write a program and no one uses it, does that program really exist?

And it's not just a matter of wasted effort. By loading up a package with programs no one necessarily wants or needs, you make it harder for anyone to find the programs that they actually do want or need. You are better off taking a minimalist approach to building your packages: build only what is needed at this point in time. Implement those requirements in the simplest, most direct manner possible (based on best practices, of course).

### Example

Gosh, there are actually a number of examples to choose from in my own toolbox. All right, how about the PLVgen package of PL/Vision? This package is a handy code generator. You can, for example, spit out function templates. You can direct the output to the screen or a file. But wait! That's not all. You can also send the generated code to a database pipe or even a "PL/SQL table" (now called an *index-by table* or *collection*). Of course, if you write the code to a PL/SQL table, you then need to extract it from that collection. It's the same with a database pipe. So the PLVgen specification ended up containing (among many other programs) the following:

```
CREATE OR REPLACE PACKAGE PLVgen
IS
   -- Direct output to a screen, file, database table, etc.

   PROCEDURE toscreen;

   PROCEDURE tofile (file IN VARCHAR2 := c_file);
```

```
PROCEDURE todbtab (tab IN VARCHAR2 := c_dbtab);

-- Pipe related functionality
PROCEDURE topipe (pipe IN VARCHAR2 := c_pipe);
PROCEDURE pipe2file (
    pipe IN VARCHAR2 := c_pipe,
    file IN VARCHAR2 := c_file);
PROCEDURE pipe2dbtab (
    pipe IN VARCHAR2 := c_pipe,
    tab IN VARCHAR2 := c_dbtab);

-- PL/SQL table related functionality
PROCEDURE topstab;
PROCEDURE pstab2file (file IN VARCHAR2 := c_file);
PROCEDURE pstab2dbtab (tab IN VARCHAR2 := c_dbtab);

    ...
END PLVgen;
```

From a purist's point of view, all this makes perfect sense. I have a strong feeling, however, that the PLVgen.pstab2dbtab program has never been (and will never be) used.

### Benefits

You don't waste time building code no one will use.

Developers can much more easily find the functionality they actually need.

### Challenges

This best practice is a sobering reminder that we are, for the most part, engaged in software development not as an art, but as a means of employment. Flights of fancy don't have much of a place in our application-development projects.

---

## PKG-09: Simplify and encourage module usage using overloading to widen calling options.

*Overloading* (also known as *static polymorphism* in the world of object-oriented languages) is the ability to create two or more programs with the same name. While you can do this in the declaration section of any PL/SQL block, it's most useful and common in package specifications.

The primary reason to overload programs in your package is to transfer the "need to know" about how to use your functionality from the user to the package itself. You anticipate the different ways that developers will want to use the packaged feature and then offer matching variations of the "same" program.

### Example

DBMS_OUTPUT.PUT_LINE ("put a line on the screen") is one of the most commonly used built-in procedures in the Oracle toolbox. It's overloaded for three types of data, as shown in the DBMS_OUTPUT specification.

```
PROCEDURE DBMS_OUTPUT.PUT_LINE (A VARCHAR2);
PROCEDURE DBMS_OUTPUT.PUT_LINE (A NUMBER);
PROCEDURE DBMS_OUTPUT.PUT_LINE (A DATE);
```

By overloading this way, Oracle allows us to pass a string, a number, or a date to this procedure, and it automatically "does the right thing." Ironically, Oracle could have provided just a single VARCHAR2 implementation, and the PL/SQL runtime engine would have implicitly converted numbers and dates to strings for us. What Oracle didn't offer was an overloading for DBMS_OUTPUT.PUT_LINE that supports the Boolean datatype, resulting in this kind of error:

```
SQL> l
  1  DECLARE
  2     l_book_is_overdue BOOLEAN;
  3  BEGIN
  4     DBMS_OUTPUT.PUT_LINE (l_book_is_overdue );
  5  END;
  6  /
ERROR
PLS-00306: wrong number or types of arguments in call to 'PUT_LINE'
```

The result is that developers often write code like this (over and over again):

```
BEGIN
    IF l_book_is_overdue
    THEN
       DBMS_OUTPUT.PUT_LINE ('TRUE');
    ELSIF NOT l_book_is_overdue
       DBMS_OUTPUT.PUT_LINE ('FALSE');
    ELSE
       DBMS_OUTPUT.PUT_LINE ('NULL');
    END IF;
```

Yuck! The point here is that it's important not only to overload programs but also to overload properly and sufficiently. You need to analyze and anticipate common developer requirements and build packages to meet those requirements. Oracle doesn't have the best track record in this regard, but you certainly can take the time and make the effort in your own programs.

### Benefits

When you overload properly, developers take your code totally for granted. They have no idea about all the work you put into your various implementations. They just know that they call "that program" and it does what's needed, regardless of variations in parameter lists.

### Challenges

Don't build your code in the abstract. Think about how the code needs to be used. Try out the usages yourself. Be ready to add to your overloadings in response to user feedback.

There are some technical limitations to overloading, for example, when combined with default parameters or when used with implicit type conversions, or even when used in different client environments (e.g., Microsoft's Active Data Objects, or ADO, doesn't recognize overloading and only "sees" the first declaration it comes across).

In situations where there are many overloadings, you might consider adding a trace so that users of the package can easily confirm which of the overloadings are being used.

### Resources

*p.sps* and *p.spb*: PL/Vision offers a substitute for DBMS_OUTPUT.PUT_LINE called the p.l procedure. This procedure is overloaded 18 times, allowing a developer to display, for example, a string and a number, a Boolean, two numbers, and so on.

## PKG-10: Consolidate the implementation of related overloaded modules.

In most cases, when you build overloaded programs, each program performs a similar operation, with variations that are usually related to different combinations of parameters. If you aren't careful about how you implement these overloadings, you will end up with a mess of code that's difficult to maintain and enhance.

The most important step you can take is to isolate behavior/features common to all overloadings and then move that common code into a separate, usually private program. All the overloadings then call that internal program.

You should also take care to organize the overloaded headers contiguously in the package specification so that they are easily identified.

### Example

Suppose that I have decided to build an encapsulation package around the book table. Developers will not write an INSERT statement to add a book; they will call an insert procedure. I can think of several different ways to perform that insert:

- Pass an individual value for each column.
- Pass a record containing a value for each column.
- Pass a collection of multiple records of book data.

Here's the package specification corresponding to these approaches:

```
CREATE OR REPLACE PACKAGE te_book
IS
    TYPE book_tt IS TABLE OF book%ROWTYPE;

    PROCEDURE ins (
        isbn_in IN book.isbn%TYPE,
        title_in IN book.title%TYPE DEFAULT NULL,
        summary_in IN book.summary%TYPE DEFAULT NULL,
        author_in IN book.author%TYPE DEFAULT NULL,
        date_published_in IN book.date_published%TYPE DEFAULT NULL,
        page_count_in IN book.page_count%TYPE DEFAULT NULL);

    --// Record-based insert //--
    PROCEDURE ins (rec_in IN book%ROWTYPE);
```

```
    --// Collection-based insert //--
    PROCEDURE ins (coll_in IN book_tt);
END te_book;
```

Here are three different programs with the same name, all with very different parameter lists. Now let's look at the package body: First, I define an "internal" insert procedure that performs the actual INSERT and provides standardized error handling and validation:

```
CREATE OR REPLACE PACKAGE BODY te_book
IS
    PROCEDURE internal_ins (
        isbn_in IN book.isbn%TYPE,
        title_in IN book.title%TYPE DEFAULT NULL,
        summary_in IN book.summary%TYPE DEFAULT NULL,
        author_in IN book.author%TYPE DEFAULT NULL,
        date_published_in IN book.date_published%TYPE DEFAULT NULL,
        page_count_in IN book.page_count%TYPE DEFAULT NULL
    )
    IS
    BEGIN
        validate_constraints;
        INSERT INTO book (
            isbn, title, summary, author, date_published, page_count)
        VALUES (
            isbn_in, title_in, summary_in, author_in,
            date_published_in, page_count_in);
    EXCEPTION
        WHEN OTHERS
        THEN
            err.log;
    END internal_ins;
```

As for my various insert procedures, I implement them either by using the internal_ins procedure directly or by calling another insert procedure, whichever is most intuitive:

```
    PROCEDURE ins (
        title_in IN book.title%TYPE DEFAULT NULL,
        summary_in IN book.summary%TYPE DEFAULT NULL,
        author_in IN book.author%TYPE DEFAULT NULL,
        date_published_in IN book.date_published%TYPE DEFAULT NULL,
        page_count_in IN book.page_count%TYPE DEFAULT NULL,
        isbn_inout IN OUT book.isbn%TYPE)
    IS
        v_pky INTEGER := new_isbn_number;
    BEGIN
        internal_ins (v_pky,
            title_in,
            summary_in,
            author_in,
            date_published_in,
            page_count_in
        );
        isbn_inout := v_pky
    END;
```

```
PROCEDURE ins (rec_in IN book%ROWTYPE) IS
BEGIN
    internal_ins (rec_in.isbn,
        rec_in.title,
        rec_in.summary,
        rec_in.author,
        rec_in.date_published,
        rec_in.page_count
    );
END;

PROCEDURE ins (coll_in IN book_tt)
IS
    indx PLS_INTEGER := coll_in.FIRST;
BEGIN
    LOOP
        EXIT WHEN indx IS NULL;

        -- Just use the record-based version
        ins (coll_in(indx));
        indx := coll_in.NEXT (indx);
    END LOOP;
END;
END;
```

### Benefits

When you need to fix or change some aspect of the implementation, you go to one place in your package body. Once the change is made, you are then sure that it will affect all overloadings.

### Challenges

Develop the discipline required to take the time to identify common areas of functionality and isolate them into their own programs.

### Resources

*te_book.pkg*: The table encapsulation package for the book table (well, just the INSERT functionality of such a package).

---

## PKG-11: Separate package specifications and bodies into different source code files.

Don't combine the specification and body of a package in the same file. Instead, store them in their own files and then, in your installation script for your product, compile all specifications first, followed by the package bodies. By taking this approach, you will find it easier to install and maintain your code base.

Over time, it's likely that your package specification will stabilize, and most changes will take place in the package body. All references to elements in a package are resolved with the specification. If the specification is recompiled, all dependent objects are marked INVALID and must be recompiled. By putting the body in its own file, you can change and recompile it without affecting the status of any other programs.

### Example

See the various *.pks* and corresponding *.pkb* files provided on the Oracle PL/SQL Best Practices web site.

You will also find a number of *.pkg* files on the site. I admit that these files violate this best practice. I decided to take this approach because they are small, self-contained packages, designed to be deployed easily in your own application environment.

PL/Vision is an example of a much more complex base of code. For this library, all package specifications and bodies are stored in their own files.

### Benefits

You can maintain and recompile packages without causing a "domino effect" that invalidates many other (unchanged) programs.

Your code will install more cleanly, since all references to packaged functionality in package bodies and standalone programs are resolved by specifications that have already been compiled.

### Challenges

Pick, and stick with, a consistent, suitable extension for package specification and body files. Most PL/SQL IDEs can be taught to recognize specific suffixes.

## PKG-12: Use a standard format for packages that include comment headers for each type of element defined in the package.

Packages are likely to be the largest, most complex code elements of your application. The internal structure of a package (both the specification and the body) is usually composed of many different types of elements, including variables, user-defined types, functions, and procedures.

Your standard package format should help you organize the elements of a package, minimize the need for forward declarations, and make it easier for you to rapidly find constructs. Make the standard format available for developers either in a template file or by generating it upon command.

### Example

Here's a template for a package body (see the "Resources" section for where to find this code):

```
CREATE OR REPLACE PACKAGE BODY name
IS
/*
PUT YOUR PACKAGE HEADER HERE
*/

/* Constants */

/* Variables */
```

```
/* Exceptions */

/* Types (records, collections, cursor variables) */

/* Private Programs */

/* Public Programs */

END name;
```

## Benefits

If everyone in your development team builds packages the same way, it will be easier to maintain the code base.

By separating code elements into distinct sections identified by headers, you can quickly find the desired code.

## Resources

*template.pks* and *template.pkb*: Template files, one for the package specification and one for the body.

*PLVgen*: Use this package of the PL/Vision library to generate a package template, either to the screen or directly to a file.

# 9

# *Built-in Packages*

Oracle provides a wide-ranging and ever-increasing set of *built-in packages*—packages that are installed into the database upon installation and that are officially supported by Oracle. These packages usually give you access to technology and features that would otherwise be difficult, if not impossible, to implement in native PL/SQL.

 You should become familiar with the built-in packages; the *Oracle Built-in Packages* book and the Oracle HTML documentation are two excellent sources for this information.

You must, however, also be careful about how you implement programs based on these packages. In many cases, the packages are somewhat hard to use and understand; hence, you should hide that complexity so that your resulting code is easy to manage over time. I recommend you follow these general guidelines:

*Encapsulate access to the built-in functionality*
I often find it very worthwhile to build my own packages on top of the Oracle packages. I can then enhance the base package's functionality. It also is then easier to use that package in a consistent fashion throughout my application.

*Read the fine print—and run your own tests—on any built-in packaged functionality*
Don't assume, just because Oracle documentation says that a program will do X, that it will, in fact, do X in your environment and your

version of Oracle. DBMS_UTILITY contains several programs, for example, that don't work as advertised (COMPILE_SCHEMA, COMMA_ TO_ TABLE, TABLE_TO_COMMA).*

# DBMS_OUTPUT

The DBMS_OUTPUT built-in package allows you to display output as your PL/SQL program executes.

## BIP-01: Avoid using the DBMS_OUTPUT.PUT_LINE procedure directly.

I am very glad that Oracle provided DBMS_OUTPUT in Version 2 of PL/SQL. Before that, it was difficult to debug code, because there was no easy way to trace program execution to the screen. However, the implementation of DBMS_ OUTPUT leaves much to be desired. Here are my complaints:

1. It's a productivity disaster. You have to type 20 characters just to ask PL/SQL to show you something.

2. The overloading is inadequate. You can pass only single strings, dates, or numbers. You can't pass it a Boolean value, nor can you pass it multiple values to be displayed (without doing the concatenation yourself).

3. If you try to display a string with more than 255 characters, you get one of two errors: ORA-20000 (a.k.a. ORU-10028 line length overflow) or ORA-06502 (numeric or value error). I don't know about you, but a whole lot of my strings are longer than 255 bytes.

4. Your program can display a maximum of 1 million lines—and it can be lots less if you forget to specify a high number in your SET SERVEROUTPUT command in SQL*Plus (resulting in an out-of-buffer error).

5. You don't see anything on your screen until your PL/SQL program has finished executing—whether that takes five minutes or five hours.

When you are faced with a utility such as DBMS_OUTPUT that is simultaneously necessary and faulty, you should say out loud (it will make you feel better):

I am fed up and I am not going to take it anymore!

Specifically, set a rule that you will never call DBMS_OUTPUT.PUT_LINE directly but instead build (or use) a layer of code over DBMS_OUTPUT.PUT_LINE that corrects most, if not all, the previously listed problems.

---

* COMPILE_SCHEMA is supposed to recompile all invalid objects. Sometimes it works, sometimes it does nothing, and sometimes it invalidates other objects as it recompiles currently invalid objects. COMMA_TO_TABLE and TABLE_TO_COMMA work with comma-delimited lists, but the elements in the list have to be valid PL/SQL identifiers. If you pass "1,2,3" to COMMA_TO_TABLE, for example, Oracle raises an exception.

## Example

You can take a number of different approaches to encapsulating and improving upon DBMS_OUTPUT.PUT_LINE. I offer implementations for each approach in the "Resources" section. They are:

- One simple procedure to display strings, dates, and numbers, and a second procedure to display Boolean values—taking care of problems 1, 2 (partly), and 3.

- A package replacement for DBMS_OUTPUT that offers a variety of overloadings of datatypes for display, such as a Boolean, a string and a Boolean, two numbers, etc. This implementation takes care of problems 1 through 4 (you can avoid buffer overflow problems when a small buffer size has been set).

- A more general trace package that hides DBMS_OUTPUT, but also allows the user to redirect the "target" of the output. If, for example, you know that you will be generating 5 MB of information, you might want to send output to a file. If your program runs for two hours, you might want to send output to a database pipe, so you can "watch" from another session.

## Benefits

You can avoid most, if not all, the nuisance problems with DBMS_OUTPUT, thus improving productivity and debugging flexibility.

## Challenges

Select a standard approach for generating output for your application, then find or build the right implementation. You can check to see if people are using the substitute by querying the ALL_SOURCE data dictionary view to check for instances of DBMS_OUTPUT.

## Resources

*pl.sp* and *bpl.sp*: Standalone procedure implementations; these are used throughout the book in place of DBMS_OUTPUT.PUT_LINE.

*p*: This package, part of PL/Vision, provides a direct package encapsulation of DBMS_OUTPUT.

*watch.pkg*: A generalized trace package with the ability to send output to a screen or database pipe.

# UTL_FILE

The UTL_FILE built-in package allows you to read and write sequential lines from a file on the same computer as the database instance from which you run your program.

## BIP-02: Improve the functionality and error handling of UTL_FILE by using a comprehensive encapsulation package.

UTL_FILE offers only the most primitive file I/O capabilities and leaves much to be desired. Here's a list of some of the things you can't do:

- Delete a file
- Obtain or change the privileges on a file
- Read or write a random line in a file (sequential operations only)
- Obtain information about directories (files in a directory, whether or not a name indicates a file or a directory, etc.)
- Define a path for finding and opening files

In addition, the way that UTL_FILE raises exceptions can make it difficult to identify and resolve file-handling errors (see **BIP-04** for details on this issue).

Ah well, we've just got to make do with what Oracle gives us, right? Wrong! You should instead create your own (or take advantage of someone else's) package that sits on top of UTL_FILE and enhances its functionality. If you don't want to go to the trouble of implementing an entire "replacement" package, you can also create alternatives to individual programs, as I demonstrate in **BIP-05**.

## *Example*

You can find one example of an encapsulation for UTL_FILE in the RevealNet Active PL/SQL Knowledge Base. This package, called PLVfile (PL/Vision file management), is implemented entirely in PL/SQL and so inherits some of the limitations of UTL_FILE. It is, however, generally easier to use and offers some added functionality, such as support for paths.

Moreover, if you are using Oracle8*i* (or above), you can now also take advantage of Java to greatly expand the possibilities of file I/O from within PL/SQL. I have created a working prototype of such an implementation. It's composed of two code elements:

*The JFile class*
> A Java class that exposes underlying Java File methods in ways that can be called from PL/SQL.

*The xfile package*
> A PL/SQL package that calls JFile methods, thereby allowing PL/SQL developers to do just about anything they need to do with files and directories—all from within PL/SQL.

The xfile specification is a superset of the UTL_FILE specification (except that it doesn't declare a record structure corresponding to UTL_FILE.FILE_TYPE). So instead of calling UTL_FILE.GET_LINE, you would call xfile.get_line. But xfile also offers much more. For example, with xfile you can delete a file, as shown:

```
did_it_work := xfile.delete ('c:\temp\garbage.dat');
```

You can also delete all the *.tmp* files in a directory:

```
xfile.delete ('/tmp/apps', '%.tmp');
```

You can also make a directory, change privileges, obtain the list of files in a directory, find out if you can read to or write from a file, and so on. As you will see if you look in the JFile code, the Java required to take these actions is absolutely minimal. The work required in PL/SQL to leverage the functionality is also light.

### Benefits

You aren't constrained by the weak implementation of file I/O offered by UTL_FILE.

### Challenges

Try to design the API of your encapsulation package to be as similar as possible to UTL_FILE (at least where there is overlap). This will make it easier for developers to "switch over"—perhaps involving just a careful global search and replace of "UTL_FILE" for "xfile," for example.

Some constraints currently can't be circumvented, such as the need to stop and restart the database to make a particular path available for file I/O (if your encapsulation relies on UTL_FILE and not Java).

### Resources

*PLVfile*: RevealNet's Active PL/SQL Knowledge Base offers this package, which enhances the functionality of the underlying UTL-FILE built-in package. Visit the PL/SQL Pipeline Archives as described in the Preface.

*JFile.java* and *xfile.pkg*: The Java-enhanced file I/O package for PL/SQL, along with the required Java class.

## BIP-03: Validate the setup of UTL_FILE with simple tests.

The hardest part about using UTL_FILE is to get it up and running. You must add one or more UTL_FILE_DIR entries in your initialization parameter file, and then restart your database to have those changes take effect.

The UTL_FILE_DIR parameter specifies those directories in which UTL_FILE can operate. The format of the parameter for file access in the *INIT.ORA* file is:

```
utl_file_dir = directory
```

Include a parameter for UTL_FILE_DIR for each directory you want to make accessible for UTL_FILE operations. The following entries, for example, enable four different directories in Unix:

```
utl_file_dir = /tmp
utl_file_dir = /ora_apps/hr/time_reporting
utl_file_dir = /ora_apps/hr/time_reporting/log
utl_file_dir = /users/test_area
```

To bypass server security and allow read/write access to all directories, you can use this special syntax:

```
utl_file_dir = *
```

Don't use this option on production systems. In a development system, this entry certainly makes it easier for developers to get up and running on UTL_FILE and test their code (but it also allows them to write "Long Live PL/SQL!" on top of your database control files!). You should, however, allow access only to a few specific directories when you move the application to production.

Here are some observations on working with and setting up accessible directories with UTL_FILE:

- Access isn't recursive through subdirectories. If the following lines were in your *INIT.ORA* file, for example:

```
utl_file_dir = c:\group\dev1
utl_file_dir = c:\group\prod\oe
utl_file_dir = c:\group\prod\ar
```

  then you couldn't open a file in the *c:\group\prod\oe\reports* subdirectory.

- Don't include the following entry in Unix systems:

```
utl_file_dir = .
```

  This allows you to read/write on the current directory in the operating system.

- Don't enclose the directory names within single or double quotes.

- In the Unix environment, a file created by UTL_FILE.FOPEN has, as its owner, the shadow process running the Oracle instance. This is usually the *oracle* owner. If you try to access these files outside of UTL_FILE, you need to have the correct privileges (or be logged in as *oracle*) to access or change these files.

- You shouldn't end your directory name with a delimiter, such as the forward slash in Unix. The following specification of a directory will result in problems when you're trying to read from or write to the directory:

```
utl_file_dir = /tmp/orafiles/ -- WILL NOT WORK!
```

After restarting your database with your UTL_FILE_DIR parameter(s), test your ability to read from and write to your desired directories, using simple test scripts (see the "Resources" section). Once you have successfully read from and written to a file, you are ready to use UTL_FILE in your application.

### Example

Here's a simple SQL*Plus script that tests UTL_FILE's ability to read from and write to a file:

```
DECLARE
    fid UTL_FILE.FILE_TYPE;
    v VARCHAR2(32767);
BEGIN
    /* Change the directory name to one to which you at least
    || THINK you have read/write access.
    */
    fid := UTL_FILE.FOPEN ('e:\demo', '&1', 'R');
    UTL_FILE.GET_LINE (fid, v);
    pl (v);
    UTL_FILE.FCLOSE (fid);

    fid := UTL_FILE.FOPEN ('e:\demo', '&2', 'W');
    UTL_FILE.PUT_LINE (fid, v);
    UTL_FILE.FCLOSE (fid);
END;
```

See "Resources" for the file containing this logic (plus the recommended exception handling).

### Benefits

You will save yourself many hours of frustrated debugging by taking these simple steps and following the basic recommendations for setting up the UTL_FILE_DIR parameter(s).

### Resources

*utlfile.tst*: A simple script to test the ability to read and write files.

## BIP-04: Handle expected and named exceptions when performing file I/O.

You may encounter a number of difficulties (and therefore exceptions) when working with operating system files. The UTL_FILE package itself offers a set of named exceptions that are specific to the package, such as UTL_FILE.INVALID_ OPERATION. (The UTL_FILE.GET_LINE procedure can also raise the standard NO_DATA_FOUND exception.) These named exceptions are all *user-defined exceptions*, which means that the SQLCODE is the same for all the exceptions: +1. For this reason, you must handle UTL_FILE exceptions by name, or you won't be able to determine which error was raised.

Every block of code that works with UTL_FILE should therefore have an exception section that: (a) traps each UTL_FILE exception by name, (b) "translates" the exception into a string that can be displayed so you can tell which error was raised, and (c) closes any opened files.

### Example

The best way to do this is to build a "local procedure" that displays error information and closes the file, as shown here:

```
IS
    fid UTL_FILE.FILE_TYPE;

    PROCEDURE recNgo (str IN VARCHAR2)
    IS
    BEGIN
        pl ('UTL_FILE error: ' || str);
        UTL_FILE.FCLOSE (fid);
    END;
BEGIN
    ... your code
EXCEPTION
    WHEN UTL_FILE.INVALID_PATH
      THEN recNgo ('invalid_path');
    WHEN UTL_FILE.INVALID_MODE
      THEN recNgo ('invalid_mode');
    WHEN UTL_FILE.INVALID_FILEHANDLE
      THEN recNgo ('invalid_filehandle');
    WHEN UTL_FILE.INVALID_OPERATION
      THEN recNgo ('invalid_operation');
    WHEN UTL_FILE.READ_ERROR
      THEN recNgo ('read_error');
    WHEN UTL_FILE.WRITE_ERROR
```

```
        THEN recNgo ('write_error');
      WHEN UTL_FILE.INTERNAL_ERROR
        THEN recNgo ('internal_error');
      WHEN OTHERS
        THEN recNgo (SQLERRM); /* TVP 9/2000 */
    END;
```

### Benefits

You can debug your UTL_FILE code more rapidly since you can immediately see what error was encountered.

Files aren't left open, which can cause "false alarms" in your code. You run your program once, and it fails (leaving the file open). You fix your program and run it again, and now your program fails because it's trying to open a file that's already open!

### Challenges

UTL_FILE also contains a procedure called FCLOSE_ALL. While this may seem a convenient choice, you must be careful in using it. Since this closes all file handles currently open in the session (even in the calling block of code), it can cause errors in sections of code that are totally unrelated to the real error.

### Resources

*utlflexc.sql*: A template of code containing a local error-handling procedure and an exception section for use with UTL_FILE.

## BIP-05: Encapsulate UTL_FILE.GET_LINE to avoid propagating the NO_DATA_FOUND exception.

UTL_FILE.GET_LINE raises the NO_DATA_FOUND exception when it reads past the end of a file (a common and even necessary "error" when you are reading the full contents of a file).

This reliance on an exception to signal EOF results in poorly structured code. Consider the following:

```
BEGIN
   LOOP
      UTL_FILE.GET_LINE (file_id, l_line);
      process_line (l_line);
   END LOOP;

   ... lots of code
EXCEPTION
   WHEN NO_DATA_FOUND
   THEN
      UTL_FILE.FCLOSE (file_id);
END;
```

The problem with this code is that the simple loop looks, for all intents and purpose, like an infinite loop. It's impossible to tell by looking at the code what makes the loop terminate. Upon termination, be sure to close the file. This logic is implemented in the exception section, which may be far away from the loop. This physical separation of logically related code can lead to a maintenance nightmare.

Instead of using UTL_FILE.GET_LINE directly, build your own "get next line" procedure and have it return a Boolean flag indicating whether the EOF was reached.

### Example

Here's a simple substitution for UTL_FILE.GET_LINE:

```
CREATE OR REPLACE PROCEDURE get_next_line (
    file_in     IN      UTL_FILE.file_type,
    line_out    OUT     VARCHAR2,
    eof_out     OUT     BOOLEAN
)
IS
BEGIN
    UTL_FILE.GET_LINE (file_in, line_out);
    eof_out := FALSE;
EXCEPTION
   WHEN NO_DATA_FOUND
   THEN
       line_out := NULL;
       eof_out := TRUE;
END;
```

Using this program, the earlier block of code becomes:

```
BEGIN
   LOOP
       get_next_line (file_id, l_line, l_eof);
       EXIT WHEN l_eof;
       process_line (l_line);
   END LOOP;
   UTL_FILE.FCLOSE (file_id);

   ... lots of code
END;
```

Now, any developer can easily see under what criteria the loop will terminate, and the file is closed immediately afterwards.

### Benefits

Your code is easier to understand and maintain. Logically related code is kept close together physically.

### Resources

*getnext.sp*: The get_next_line procedure replaces UTL_FILE.GET_LINE.

---

## BIP-06: Soft-code directory names in your calls to UTL_FILE.FOPEN.

Oracle requires that you pass the directory name along with the filename when you open a file. The tendency among developers is to place these directory names directly in the call to UTL_FILE.FOPEN, thinking that the locations of files will not change or not really envisioning an alternative. A directory name is just one example of an operating system dependency within PL/SQL code, and you should make every effort to isolate such dependencies from your business logic.

There are several distinct approaches to avoiding such hard-coding:

- Store directory names in a database table. Instead of calling UTL_FILE.FOPEN directly, call your own file open function that obtains the directory from the table, based on various characteristics, such as instance name, development phase, application component, etc.

- Obtain the current settings for UTL_FILE_DIR (the allowable directories for read/write activity) and then extract your directory from that string. This is possible if you can identify the needed directory from its name.

- Add support for a path in UTL_FILE, in which you define a list of directories from which a file may be read. Again, provide your own encapsulation of UTL_FILE.FOPEN that reads from the path list instead of a static, single directory.

The following example demonstrates each technique.

### Example

First, let's take a look at "soft coding" directory names in a database table (I will not show all the code here; see the "Resources" section for the relevant file references). I want to change directories according to phase of development and the application with which I am working. I create a table:

```
CREATE TABLE dir (
    phase INTEGER,
    app VARCHAR2(100),
    name VARCHAR2(100));
```

and then within my *fdir* package create an encapsulation of UTL_FILE.FOPEN as follows:

```
FUNCTION fopen (
    app_in    IN    dir.app%TYPE,
    file_in   IN    VARCHAR2,
    mode_in   IN    VARCHAR2 := 'R'
)
    RETURN UTL_FILE.file_type
IS
    retval   UTL_FILE.file_type;
    l_name   dir.name%TYPE;
BEGIN
    l_name := fdir.name (app_in);

    IF l_name IS NOT NULL
    THEN
        retval := UTL_FILE.fopen (l_name, file_in, mode_in);
    END IF;

    RETURN retval;
END fopen;
```

where fdir.name retrieves the name for an application. The phase of development is set as a global variable, since I don't want my actual code to contain references to the phase.

With the package in place, I can set the phase to "development" in my current session as follows:

```
EXEC fdir.setphase (fdir.c_dev);
```

And then all calls to fdir.open will automatically use the development directory for whatever application I specify. Here's an example:

```
DECLARE
    fid       UTL_FILE.file_type;
    l_line    VARCHAR2 (100);
BEGIN
    fid := fdir.fopen ('LIBMEM', 'fdir.txt');
    UTL_FILE.get_line (fid, l_line);
    pl (l_line);
    UTL_FILE.fclose (fid);
END;
/
```

You can also obtain the value for the UTL_FILE_DIR parameter used in your database initialization file either by querying from the V$PARAMETER file:

```
SELECT value
  FROM v$parameter
 WHERE name = 'utl_file_dir';
```

or by calling DBMS_UTILITY.GET_PARAMETER_VALUE (available in Oracle8*i* and above). See *dbparm.pkg* for an example of how to use this built-in.

Finally, if you want to explore adding a path to your UTL_FILE open operation, check out the *filepath* package (see "Resources").

### Benefits

You can more easily port your code from development to test to production, or to different operation systems/hardware platforms.

You can change the locations of files in your application without having to change your code.

### Challenges

Set the rules for opening files before you start building your application code. Create a package that implements the rules, and make sure everyone uses that package. You can check for compliance with the rule by using the *valstd.pkg* package listed in the "Resources" section, along with the following call:

```
SQL> exec valstd.progwith ('UTL_FILE.FOPEN')
```

### Resources

*fdir.pkg* and *fdir.tst*: A package that allows you to define directories in a table based on development phase and application, and then open files without hardcoding the directory location. There is also an accompanying test script.

*filepath.pkg*: An encapsulation of UTL_FILE.FOPEN that adds support for a user-specified path (it can only be used to open files in Read mode).

*valstd.pkg*: A general (and simple) standards validation package that searches ALL_SOURCE for the specified string and reports on those programs that contain the string.

# DBMS_PIPE

Use the DBMS_PIPE built-in package to create, write to, and read from database pipes. *Database pipes* are chunks of memory in the System Global Area that serve as conduits of information, primarily between Oracle sessions. Since the information is stored in memory, all information in a pipe is lost when a database is shut down.

Prior to Oracle8 and Oracle8*i*, database pipes were used to build "a better debugger" (better than DBMS_OUTPUT, in any case) and, among other activities, interact with native operating system programs. The external program could then perform tasks that would otherwise be impossible from within PL/SQL.

## BIP-07: Encapsulate interaction with specific pipes.

A pipe is identified by its name: a string of up to 128 characters. Messages that are written to, and read from, a pipe can be composed of one or more "packets," and each message can be made up of different numbers and types of packets (for example, two strings and a number or 12 dates). Working with a pipe can raise both pipe-specific and general errors.

For all these reasons, whenever you are working with a database pipe (or pipes), you should encapsulate access to that pipe behind a package interface. Make sure that no user of a pipe hard-codes the name of the pipe in his logic. Avoid the explicit packing and unpacking of message contents; instead, call procedures to do that work for you and for any other developer.

### Example

Here's an example of a pipe encapsulation package around the book table:

```
CREATE OR REPLACE PACKAGE pe_book

-- Wrapper around pipe based on book

-- NOTE: EXECUTE authority on DBMS_LOCK is required.
--    Issue this command from SYS:
--    GRANT EXECUTE ON DBMS_LOCK TO PUBLIC;

IS
    c_name   CONSTANT VARCHAR2 (200) := 'BOOK_pipe';

/* Overloadings of send */

    PROCEDURE send (
        isbn_in           IN book.isbn%TYPE DEFAULT NULL,
        title_in          IN book.title%TYPE DEFAULT NULL,
```

```
             summary_in          IN book.summary%TYPE DEFAULT NULL,
             author_in           IN book.author%TYPE DEFAULT NULL,
             date_published_in   IN book.date_published%TYPE DEFAULT NULL,
             page_count_in       IN book.page_count%TYPE DEFAULT NULL,
             wait                IN INTEGER := 0
          );

       PROCEDURE send (rec_in IN book%ROWTYPE, wait IN INTEGER := 0);

   /* Overloadings of receive */

       PROCEDURE receive (
          isbn_out             OUT book.isbn%TYPE,
          title_out            OUT book.title%TYPE,
          summary_out          OUT book.summary%TYPE,
          author_out           OUT book.author%TYPE,
          date_published_out   OUT book.date_published%TYPE,
          page_count_out       OUT book.page_count%TYPE,
          wait                 IN  INTEGER := 0
          );

       PROCEDURE receive (
          rec_out    OUT  book%ROWTYPE,
          wait       IN   INTEGER := 0
          );
    END pe_book;
```

With this package in place, I can easily write the contents of a record to a pipe:

```
DECLARE
    book_rec book%ROWTYPE;
BEGIN
    book_rec := last_book_reserved;
    pe_book.send (book_rec);
```

I leave it to the package to do all the hard work; I don't even have to know the name of the pipe; heck, I don't even have to know how DBMS_PIPE works! And if the pipe name needs to change or even if a column is added to the book table, this code doesn't have to be modified at all.

### Benefits

Users of the pipe encapsulation package can concentrate on the logical work they want to accomplish, rather than on the details of managing pipes. This improves developer productivity and the resulting quality of their code.

### Challenges

The biggest challenge is to build these packages. It can take lots of work, especially if you are encapsulating a table with lots of columns. You should investigate ways to *generate,* rather than write such code. See **DEV-05** for code generation options.

### Resources

*pe_book.pkg*: The full implementation of the pipe encapsulation package for the book table.

## BIP-08: *Provide explicit and appropriate timeout values when you send and receive messages.*

When you send or receive a message via a database pipe, you can specify how long you are willing to wait for the operation to succeed. A pipe might be full, which means that you can't immediately send to that pipe. A pipe might be empty, which means that you can't immediately receive a message from that pipe.

The default wait time for DBMS_PIIPE is 86.4 million seconds, otherwise known as 1,000 days. This is an awfully long time wait for an operation to complete, and could cause problems in your application. You should never rely on the default timeout values in any DBMS_PIPE calls. Always provide an override.

### Example

Here's the implementation of the pe_book.send procedure:

```
PROCEDURE pe_book.receive (
    isbn_out              OUT       book.isbn%TYPE,
    title_out             OUT       book.title%TYPE,
    summary_out           OUT       book.summary%TYPE,
    author_out            OUT       book.author%TYPE,
    date_published_out    OUT       book.date_published%TYPE,
    page_count_out        OUT       book.page_count%TYPE,
    wait                  IN        INTEGER := 0
)
IS
BEGIN
    -- Receive next message and unpack for each column.
    g_status := DBMS_PIPE.receive_message (defname, wait);

    IF g_status = 0
    THEN
       DBMS_PIPE.unpack_message (isbn_out);
       DBMS_PIPE.unpack_message (title_out);
       DBMS_PIPE.unpack_message (summary_out);
       DBMS_PIPE.unpack_message (author_out);
       DBMS_PIPE.unpack_message (date_published_out);
       DBMS_PIPE.unpack_message (page_count_out);
    END IF;

    g_action := 'RECEIVE_MESSAGE';
END;
```

In this case, I always override the default wait time with the value passed in by the wait parameter. The default value on wait is 0 seconds (immediate success required or it times out), but it can be overridden by a user of the package.

### Benefits

You can avoid having your application appear frozen as it waits virtually forever for a "green light" from the pipe.

### Challenges

Your code to handle the lack of a message on the pipe needs to be just as robust as the code to handle a valid message. This may not be a valid condition depending on your application, but should always be handled.

### Resources

*pe_book.pkg*: The full implementation of the pipe encapsulation package for the book table.

---

## BIP-09: Use RESET_BUFFER in exception handlers and before you pack data into the message buffer.

Each session connected to Oracle has a message buffer that can contain up to 4096 bytes of information. You can place data into the buffer with calls to DBMS_PIPE.PACK_MESSAGE and DBMS_PIPE.RECEIVE_MESSAGE.

Prior to packing data into the buffer, you should not assume it's empty. Your last unpack operation might have left some data in the buffer, or a previous pack-and-send operation could have failed with an exception. For these reasons, you should call DBMS_PIPE.RESET_BUFFER both before you pack data into the message buffer and in exception handlers in blocks where the buffer may have been partially filled.

### Example

The pipe encapsulation package for the book table, pe_book, offers this implementation of the send operation:

```
PROCEDURE pe_book.send (
    isbn_in             IN    book.isbn%TYPE DEFAULT NULL,
    title_in            IN    book.title%TYPE DEFAULT NULL,
    summary_in          IN    book.summary%TYPE DEFAULT NULL,
    author_in           IN    book.author%TYPE DEFAULT NULL,
    date_published_in   IN    book.date_published%TYPE DEFAULT NULL,
    page_count_in       IN    book.page_count%TYPE DEFAULT NULL,
    wait                IN    INTEGER := 0
)
IS
BEGIN
    -- Clear the buffer before writing.
    DBMS_PIPE.reset_buffer;

    -- For each column, pack item into buffer.
    DBMS_PIPE.pack_message (isbn_in);
    DBMS_PIPE.pack_message (title_in);
    DBMS_PIPE.pack_message (summary_in);
    DBMS_PIPE.pack_message (author_in);
    DBMS_PIPE.pack_message (date_published_in);
    DBMS_PIPE.pack_message (page_count_in);

    -- Send the message
    g_status :=
        DBMS_PIPE.send_message (defname, NVL (wait, g_sendwait));
```

```
     g_action := 'SEND_MESSAGE';
EXCEPTION
   WHEN OTHERS
   THEN
      DBMS_PIPE.reset_buffer;
      RAISE;
END;
```

The first step taken is a resetting of the buffer. If you don't do this, it's quite possible for the buffer to have a previous set of book information that was never sent, or some other data. Finally, the exception section makes sure to empty out the buffer before re-raising the same exception.

### Benefits

The contents in the database pipe are more dependable, leading to a higher likelihood of correct program behavior.

### Resources

*pe_book.pkg*: The full implementation of the pipe encapsulation package for the book table.

# DBMS_JOB

The DBMS_JOB built-in package offers an API into an Oracle subsystem known as the *job queue*. The Oracle job queue allows for the scheduling and execution of PL/SQL routines (*jobs*) at predefined times and/or repeated job execution at regular intervals. DBMS_JOB provides programs for submitting and executing jobs, changing job execution parameters, and removing or temporarily suspending job execution. And that's all great, but DBMS_JOB has several key weaknesses, including:

- Little or no job management features. A job is assigned an ID number, but you can't give your job a name, which makes it hard to locate and manage the job after submission.

- Scheduling the frequency of execution can be complicated process. If you want a job to run every Monday, Wednesday, and Friday at noon, for example, you need to pass the following string to DBMS_JOB.SUBMIT:

```
'TRUNC(LEAST(NEXT_DAY,(SYSDATE, ''MONDAY''),
            NEXT_DAY(,(SYSDATE, ''WEDNESDAY''),
            NEXT_DAY(,(SYSDATE, ''FRIDAY''))) + 1/2'
```

As with the other built-in packages discussed in this chapter, you can overcome such weaknesses by building your own layer of code around the DBMS_JOB procedures.

## BIP-10: Use your own submission procedure to improve job management capabilities.

As noted earlier, there's no way to assign a name to a job with DBMS_JOB. A job name comes in very handy for a number of purposes, including easy analysis of job status and a way to handle jobs that fail.

Rather than call DBMS_JOB.SUBMIT directly, you should build an encapsulation around that procedure, which submits the job, but also keep track of additional job information.

### Example

The *myJob* package (see the "Resources" section) offers a simple encapsulation of DBMS_JOB submit that also populates a database table with additional job information (in this case, only the name of the job).

Here's the submit procedure:

```
FUNCTION myJob.submit (
    name_in      IN    job.name%TYPE,
    what_in      IN    job.what%TYPE,
    next_date_in IN    DATE := SYSDATE,
    interval_in  IN    job.interval%TYPE := NULL
)
    RETURN job.id%TYPE
IS
    retval    job.id%TYPE;
BEGIN
    DBMS_JOB.submit (retval, what_in, next_date_in, interval_in
    );

    INSERT INTO job
            (id, name, what, next_date, interval)
        VALUES (
            retval, name_in, what_in, next_date_in, interval_in
        );

    COMMIT;
    RETURN retval;
END submit;
```

Now that this information is available to me, you can use it in your other procedures. You can, for example, now remove a job by name:

```
BEGIN
    myJob.remove ('weekly_analysis');
```

Most important, you can reference the job by name within the exception section of the job's stored procedure, which is crucial for managing jobs that fail (see **BIP-11**).

The myJob.submit procedure also performs a COMMIT after submitting the job and inserting the job information into my job table. You should always COMMIT after a call to DBMS_JOB.SUBMIT, especially if you want your job to execute immediately.

### Benefits

It's much easier to manage a job when you can give a name that is meaningful in the context of your application.

### Challenges

Ensure that all developers know about and use the job encapsulation code. And, of course, you need to build the package as well!

### Resources

*myjob.pkg*: A prototype package that demonstrates how to give a name to a job and then manage that job by name.

*PLVjob*: The Active PL/SQL Knowledge Base of RevealNet includes the PLVjob package, which offers many additional features for DBMS_JOB users. You can manage jobs by name and also schedule jobs through a variety of means, including *cron* syntax.

## BIP-11: Trap all errors in DBMS_JOB-executed stored procedures and modify the job queue accordingly.

Oracle keeps track of the number of times a job fails (raises an unhandled exception); once it fails 16 times, the job is marked as "broken." That's handy, but not very practical. If a job breaks once, it will probably break again. More importantly, though, the DBA should be made aware of a job failure so that the code (or the execution environment) can be modified to allow the job to run successfully.

You can improve upon DBMS_JOB by trapping all errors that occur in your job blocks and stored procedure calls. Immediately mark the job as broken, so that Oracle doesn't try to run the job again and again, and send out an alert of some sort so that the job can be fixed.

### Example

Now the *myJob* package will come in handy. With *myJob*, I can assign a name to a job and use that name to obtain the job ID number. This means that I can write an exception section in my stored procedure like this:

```
CREATE OR REPLACE PROCEDURE calculate_overdue_fines (...)
IS
    c_program CONSTANT VARCHAR2(30) :=
        'calculate_overdue_fines';
BEGIN
    ...
EXCEPTION
```

```
WHEN OTHERS
THEN
    myJob.broken (myJob.id (c_program);
    dba_beeper.notify (c_program, SQLERRM);
END;
```

Note that I don't offer an implementation of the dba_beeper.notify procedure!

## Benefits

Following this best practice will help you avoid repetitive, failed executions of jobs.

You can also repair broken jobs more quickly.

## Challenges

Ensure that all developers know about and use the job encapsulation package in error handlers. And, of course, you need to build the package as well!

## Resources

*myjob.pkg*: A prototype package that demonstrates how to give a name to a job and then manage that job by name.

# A

# *Best Practices*
# *Quick Reference*

This appendix compiles the best practice titles across all the chapters into a concise reference. Once you have studied the individual best practices, you can use this appendix as a checklist, to be reviewed before you begin coding a new program or application.

You can also find a removable version of this quick reference bound into the back of the book.

## 1. The Development Process

DEV-01:  Set standards and guidelines before writing any code.
DEV-02:  Ask for help after 30 minutes on a problem.
DEV-03:  Walk through each other's code.
DEV-04:  Validate standards against source code in the database.
DEV-05:  Generate code whenever possible and appropriate.
DEV-06:  Set up and use formal unit testing procedures.
DEV-07:  Use independent testers for functional sign-off.

## 2. Coding Style and Conventions

STYL-01:  Adopt a consistent, readable format that is easy to maintain.
STYL-02:  Adopt logical, consistent naming conventions for modules and data structures.
STYL-03:  Standardize module and program headers.
STYL-04:  Tag module END statements with module names.
STYL-05:  Name procedures with verb phrases and functions with noun phrases.
STYL-06:  Self-document using block and loop labels.
STYL-07:  Express complex expressions unambiguously using parentheses.

STYL-08: Use vertical code alignment to emphasize vertical relationships.
STYL-09: Comment tersely with value-added information.
STYL-10: Adopt meaningful naming conventions for source files.

## 3. Variables and Data Structures

### Declaring Variables and Data Structures

DAT-01: Match datatypes to computational usage.
DAT-02: Anchor variables to database datatypes using %TYPE and %ROWTYPE.
DAT-03: Use SUBTYPE to standardize application-specific datatypes.
DAT-04: Do not hard-code VARCHAR2 lengths.
DAT-05: Use CONSTANT declarations for variables whose values do not change.
DAT-06: Perform complex variable initialization in the executable section.

### Using Variables and Data Structures

DAT-07: Replace complex expressions with Boolean variables and functions.
DAT-08: Do not overload data structure usage.
DAT-09: Remove unused variables and code.
DAT-10: Clean up data structures when your program terminates (successfully or with an error).
DAT-11: Beware of and avoid implicit datatype conversions.

### Declaring and Using Package Variables

DAT-12: Package application-named literal constants together.
DAT-13: Centralize TYPE definitions in package specifications.
DAT-14: Use package globals judiciously and only in package bodies.
DAT-15: Expose package globals using "get and set" modules.

## 4. Control Structures

### Conditional and Boolean Logic

CTL-01: Use ELSIF with mutually exclusive clauses.
CTL-02: Use IF...ELSIF only to test a single, simple condition.
CTL-03: Replace and simplify IF statements with Boolean expressions.

### Loop Processing

CTL-04: Never EXIT or RETURN from WHILE and FOR loops.
CTL-05: Use a single EXIT in simple loops.
CTL-06: Use a simple loop to avoid redundant code required by a WHILE loop.
CTL-07: Never declare the FOR loop index.
CTL-08: Scan collections using FIRST, LAST, and NEXT in loops.
CTL-09: Move static expressions outside of loops and SQL statements.

### Miscellaneous

CTL-10: Use anonymous blocks within IF statements to conserve resources.
CTL-11: Label and highlight GOTOs if using this normally unnecessary construct.

## 5. Exception Handling

EXC-00: Set guidelines for application-wide error handling before you start coding.

### Raising Exceptions

EXC-01: Verify preconditions using standardized assertion routines that raise violation exceptions.

EXC-02: Use the default exception-handling model to communicate module status back to calling PL/SQL programs.

EXC-03: Catch all exceptions and convert to meaningful return codes before returning to non-PL/SQL host programs.

EXC-04: Use your own raise procedure in place of explicit calls to RAISE_APPLICATION_ERROR.

EXC-05: Only RAISE exceptions for errors, not to branch execution control.

EXC-06: Do not overload an exception with multiple errors unless the loss of information is intentional.

### Handling Exceptions

EXC-07: Handle exceptions that cannot be avoided but can be anticipated.

EXC-08: Avoid hard-coded exposure of error handling by using standard, declarative procedures.

EXC-09: Use named constants to soft-code application-specific error numbers and messages.

EXC-10: Include standardized modules in packages to dump package state when errors occur.

EXC-11: Use WHEN OTHERS only for unknown exceptions that need to be trapped.

### Declaring Exceptions

EXC-12: Standardize named application exceptions in package specifications.

EXC-13: Document all package exceptions by module in package specifications.

EXC-14: Use the EXCEPTION_INIT pragma to name system exceptions that might be raised by your program.

## 6. Writing SQL in PL/SQL

SQL-00: Establish and follow clear rules for how to write SQL in your application.

### General SQL and Transaction Management

SQL-01: Qualify PL/SQL variables with their scope names when referenced inside SQL statements.

SQL-02: Use incremental COMMITs to avoid rollback segment errors when changing large numbers of rows.

SQL-03: Use autonomous transactions to isolate the effect of COMMITs and ROLLBACKs (Oracle8*i*).

### Querying Data from PL/SQL

SQL-04:  Put single-row fetches inside functions; never hard-code a query in your block.

SQL-05:  Hide reliance on the dual table.

SQL-06:  Define multi-row cursors in packages so they can be used from multiple programs.

SQL-07:  Fetch into cursor records, never into a hard-coded list of variables.

SQL-08:  Use COUNT only when the actual number of occurrences is needed.

SQL-09:  Use a cursor FOR loop to fetch all rows in a cursor unconditionally.

SQL-10:  Never use a cursor FOR loop to fetch just one row.

SQL-11:  Specify columns to be updated in a SELECT FOR UPDATE statement.

SQL-12:  Parameterize explicit cursors.

SQL-13:  Use RETURNING to retrieve information about modified rows (Oracle8).

SQL-14:  Use BULK COLLECT to improve performance of multi-row queries (Oracle8*i*).

### Changing Data from PL/SQL

SQL-15:  Encapsulate INSERT, UPDATE and DELETE statements behind procedure calls.

SQL-16:  Reference cursor attributes immediately after executing the SQL operation.

SQL-17:  Check SQL%ROWCOUNT when updating or removing data that "should" be there.

SQL-18:  Use FORALL to improve performance of collection-based DML (Oracle8*i*).

### Dynamic SQL and Dynamic PL/SQL

SQL-19:  Encapsulate dynamic SQL parsing to improve error detection and cleanup.

SQL-20:  Bind, do not concatenate, variable values into dynamic SQL strings.

SQL-21:  Soft-code the maximum length of columns in DBMS_SQL.DEFINE_COLUMN calls.

SQL-22:  Apply the invoker rights method to all stored code that executes dynamic SQL (Oracle8*i*).

SQL-23:  Standardize the format of complex dynamic SQL strings.

---

## 7. Program Construction

### Structure and Parameters

MOD-01:  Encapsulate and name business rules and formulas behind function headers.

MOD-02:  Standardize module structure using function and procedure templates.

MOD-03:  Limit execution section sizes to a single page using modularization.

MOD-04:  Use named notation to clarify, self-document, and simplify module calls.

MOD-05:  Avoid side-effects in your programs.

MOD-06:  Use NOCOPY to minimize overhead when collections and records are [IN] OUT parameters (Oracle8*i*).

### Functions

MOD-07: Limit functions to a single RETURN statement in the execution section.

MOD-08: Keep functions pure by avoiding [IN] OUT parameters.

MOD-09: Never return NULL from Boolean functions.

### Triggers

MOD-10: Minimize the size of trigger execution section sizes.

MOD-11: Consolidate "overlapping" DML triggers to control execution order.

MOD-12: Raise exceptions to report on do-nothing INSTEAD OF triggers.

MOD-13: Implement server problem logs and "to do" lists using database triggers.

MOD-14: Use ORA_% public synonyms to reference database and schema event trigger attributes.

MOD-15: Validate complex business rules with DML triggers.

MOD-16: Populate columns of derived values with triggers.

MOD-17: Use operational directives to provide more meaningful error messages from within triggers.

---

## 8. Package Construction

PKG-01: Group related data structures and functionality together in a single package.

PKG-02: Provide well-defined interfaces to business data and functional manipulation using packages.

PKG-03: Freeze and build package specifications before implementing package bodies.

PKG-04: Implement flexible, user-adjustable functionality using package state toggles and related techniques.

PKG-05: Build trace "windows" into your packages using standardized programs.

PKG-06: Use package body persistent data structures to cache and optimize data-driven processing.

PKG-07: Insulate applications from Oracle version sensitivity using version-specific implementations.

PKG-08: Avoid bloating package code with unnecessary but easy-to-build modules.

PKG-09: Simplify and encourage module usage using overloading to widen calling options.

PKG-10: Consolidate the implementation of related overloaded modules.

PKG-11: Separate package specifications and bodies into different source code files.

PKG-12: Use a standard format for packages that include comment headers for each type of element defined in the package.

## 9. Built-in Packages

### DBMS_OUTPUT

BIP-01:    Avoid using the DBMS_OUTPUT.PUT_LINE procedure directly.

### UTL_FILE

BIP-02:    Improve the functionality and error handling of UTL_FILE by using a comprehensive encapsulation package.

BIP-03:    Validate the setup of UTL_FILE with simple tests.

BIP-04:    Handle expected and named exceptions when performing file I/O.

BIP-05:    Encapsulate UTL_FILE.GET_LINE to avoid propagating the NO_DATA_FOUND exception.

BIP-06:    Soft-code directory names in your calls to UTL_FILE.FOPEN

### DBMS_PIPE

BIP-07:    Encapsulate interaction with specific pipes.

BIP-08:    Provide explicit and appropriate timeout values when you send and receive messages.

BIP-09:    Use RESET_BUFFER in exception handlers and before you pack data into the message buffer.

### DBMS_JOB

BIP-10:    Use your own submission procedures to improve job management capabilities.

BIP-11:    Trap all errors in DBMS_JOB-executed stored procedures and modify the job queue accordingly.

# About the Author

**Steven Feuerstein** is considered one of the world's leading experts on the Oracle PL/SQL language. He is the author or coauthor of *Oracle PL/SQL Programming, Oracle PL/SQL Programming: Guide to Oracle8i Features, Oracle PL/SQL Developer's Workbook, Oracle Built-in Packages, Advanced Oracle PL/SQL Programming with Packages,* and several pocket reference books (all from O'Reilly & Associates). Steven is a Senior Technology Advisor with Quest Software, has been developing software since 1980, and worked for Oracle Corporation from 1987 to 1992.

Steven hosts the PL/SQL Pipeline, an online community for PL/SQL developers (*http://www.revealnet.com/Pipelines/PLSQL/index.htm*) and contributes to Reveal-Net's Active PL/SQL Knowledge Base. He offers training and consulting on software development and the Oracle PL/SQL language through PL/Solutions (*http://www.plsolutions.com*).

In matters pertaining to humanity rather than programming, Steven currently serves as president of the Board of Directors of the Crossroads Fund, which makes grants to Chicagoland organizations working for social, racial, environmental, and economic justice (*http://www.CrossroadsFund.org*). He is also active in Not In My Name, a gathering of Jews who seek a lasting and just peace between Israelis and Palestinians (*http://www.nimn.org*). You can reach Steven at *steven@stevenfeuerstein.com*.

# Colophon

Our look is the result of reader comments, our own experimentation, and feedback from distribution channels. Distinctive covers complement our distinctive approach to technical topics, breathing personality and life into potentially dry subjects.

The animal on the cover of *Oracle PL/SQL Best Practices* is a red wood ant. Red wood ants (*Formica aquilonia*) are often the dominant ants of forests throughout the northern hemisphere. *F. aquilonia* can build nest mounds of dried spruce needles and twigs that are three feet or more in diameter and height. Each nest can contain thousands of ants as well as several queens. The insects have no sting but can defend themselves by firing formic acid from their rear ends when disturbed.

The workers vary in size up to about 1/2 inch in length with a red thorax, black abdomen, and red and black marked head. The ants are both scavengers and general predators of insects, carrying many soft-bodied caterpillars, flies, and sawflies along their several major trails back to the nest.

Red wood ants are a keystone species (i.e., without them the ecosystem changes fundamentally). When red ants disappear from a system, herbivorous insects can subsequently damage forest trees. In forests weakened by pollution and acid rain in central Europe, red wood ant populations are often endangered, which in turn causes further imbalances in predator-prey dynamics and the ecosystem. These rare ants are protected by law in some European countries because of their great value in destroying forest pests.

For 28 years, Professor Seigo Higashi has been studying a supercolony of Japanese red wood ants (*Formica yessensis*), which dwell along a strip of shoreline on the Ishikari coast of northern Japan. When first discovered in 1973, the colony consisted of approximately 45,000 nests with connecting tunnels extending nearly 12.4 miles along the shore of the Japan Sea. It was estimated that the colony had about 306 million workers and 1.1 million queens, and is thought to be about 1,000 years old. Since 1973, the colony has been under siege, threatened by the development of infrastructure for a new port on Ishikari Bay, which has occurred on top of 30% of the ant megalopolis. This has reduced the number of red wood ants living there by more than half.

The Ishikari ants are one of only two known ant supercolonies in the world. The other, smaller one is in the Swiss Jura mountains.

Mary Anne Weeks Mayo was the production editor, and Clairemarie Fisher O'Leary was the copyeditor for *Oracle PL/SQL Best Practices*. Mary Sheehan, Matt Hutchinson, and Jane Ellin provided quality control. Rachel Wheeler and Gabe Weiss provided production assistance.

Ellie Volckhausen designed the cover of this book, based on a series design by Edie Freedman. The cover image is a 19th-century engraving from the Dover Pictorial Archive. Emma Colby produced the cover layout with QuarkXPress 4.1 using Adobe's ITC Garamond font.

David Futato designed the interior layout based on a series design by Nancy Priest. Clifford Dyer and Anne-Marie Vaduva converted the files from Microsoft Word to FrameMaker 5.5.6 using tools created by Mike Sierra. The text and heading fonts are ITC Garamond Light and Garamond Book. This colophon was compiled by Mary Anne Weeks Mayo.

Whenever possible, our books use a durable and flexible lay-flat binding. If the page count exceeds this binding's limit, perfect binding is used.

# Oracle

## Oracle PL/SQL Built-ins Pocket Reference

*By Steven Feuerstein,*
*John Beresniewicz & Chip Dawes*
*1st Edition October 1998*
*78 pages, ISBN 1-56592-456-8*

This companion quick reference to
Steven Feuerstein's bestselling *Oracle*
*PL/SQL Programming* and *Oracle*
*Built-in Packages* will help you use
Oracle's extensive set of built-in functions
and packages, including those new
to Oracle8. You'll learn how to call
numeric, character, date, conversion, large object (LOB), and
miscellaneous functions, as well as packages like DBMS_SQL
and DBMS_OUTPUT.

## Oracle PL/SQL Developer's Workbook

*By Steven Feuerstein*
*with Andrew Odewahn*
*1st Edition May 2000*
*592 pages, ISBN 1-56592-674-9*

A companion to Feuerstein's other
bestselling Oracle PL/SQL books,
this workbook contains a carefully
constructed set of problems and
solutions that will test your language
skills and help you become a better developer. Exercises
are provided at three levels: beginner, intermediate, and
expert. It covers the full set of language features: variables,
loops, exception handling, data structures, object technology,
cursors, built-in functions and packages, PL/SQL tuning, and
the new Oracle8i features (including Java and the Web).

# How to stay in touch with O'Reilly

## 1. Visit Our Award-Winning Site

*http://www.oreilly.com/*

★ "Top 100 Sites on the Web" —*PC Magazine*
★ "Top 5% Web sites" —*Point Communications*
★ "3-Star site" —*The McKinley Group*

Our web site contains a library of comprehensive product information (including book excerpts and tables of contents), downloadable software, background articles, interviews with technology leaders, links to relevant sites, book cover art, and more. File us in your Bookmarks or Hotlist!

## 2. Join Our Email Mailing Lists

### New Product Releases

To receive automatic email with brief descriptions of all new O'Reilly products as they are released, send email to:
**ora-news-subscribe@lists.oreilly.com**
Put the following information in the first line of your message (*not* in the Subject field):
**subscribe ora-news**

### O'Reilly Events

If you'd also like us to send information about trade show events, special promotions, and other O'Reilly events, send email to:
**ora-news-subscribe@lists.oreilly.com**
Put the following information in the first line of your message (*not* in the Subject field):
**subscribe ora-events**

## 3. Get Examples from Our Books via FTP

There are two ways to access an archive of example files from our books:

### Regular FTP

- ftp to:
  **ftp.oreilly.com**
  (login: anonymous
  password: your email address)
- Point your web browser to:
  **ftp://ftp.oreilly.com/**

### FTPMAIL

- Send an email message to:
  **ftpmail@online.oreilly.com**
  (Write "help" in the message body)

## 4. Contact Us via Email

**order@oreilly.com**
To place a book or software order online. Good for North American and international customers.

**subscriptions@oreilly.com**
To place an order for any of our newsletters or periodicals.

**books@oreilly.com**
General questions about any of our books.

**software@oreilly.com**
For general questions and product information about our software. Check out O'Reilly Software Online at **http://software.oreilly.com/** for software and technical support information. Registered O'Reilly software users send your questions to:
**website-support@oreilly.com**

**cs@oreilly.com**
For answers to problems regarding your order or our products.

**booktech@oreilly.com**
For book content technical questions or corrections.

**proposals@oreilly.com**
To submit new book or software proposals to our editors and product managers.

**international@oreilly.com**
For information about our international distributors or translation queries. For a list of our distributors outside of North America check out:
**http://www.oreilly.com/distributors.html**

## 5. Work with Us

Check out our website for current employment opportunites:
**http://jobs.oreilly.com/**

O'Reilly & Associates, Inc.
101 Morris Street, Sebastopol, CA 95472 USA
TEL    707-829-0515 or 800-998-9938
           (6am to 5pm PST)
FAX    707-829-0104

## O'REILLY®

# International Distributors

## UK, EUROPE, MIDDLE EAST AND AFRICA (EXCEPT FRANCE, GERMANY, AUSTRIA, SWITZERLAND, LUXEMBOURG, AND LIECHTENSTEIN)

**INQUIRIES**
O'Reilly UK Limited
4 Castle Street
Farnham
Surrey, GU9 7HS
United Kingdom
Telephone: 44-1252-711776
Fax: 44-1252-734211
Email: information@oreilly.co.uk

**ORDERS**
Wiley Distribution Services Ltd.
1 Oldlands Way
Bognor Regis
West Sussex PO22 9SA
United Kingdom
Telephone: 44-1243-843294
UK Freephone: 0800-243207
Fax: 44-1243-843302 (Europe/EU orders)
or 44-1243-843274 (Middle East/Africa)
Email: cs-books@wiley.co.uk

## GERMANY, SWITZERLAND, AUSTRIA, LUXEMBOURG, AND LIECHTENSTEIN

**INQUIRIES & ORDERS**
O'Reilly Verlag
Balthasarstr. 81
D-50670 Köln, Germany
Telephone: 49-221-973160-91
Fax: 49-221-973160-8
Email: anfragen@oreilly.de (inquiries)
Email: order@oreilly.de (orders)

## FRANCE

**INQUIRIES & ORDERS**
Éditions O'Reilly
18 rue Séguier
75006 Paris, France
Tel: 1-40-51-71-89
Fax: 1-40-51-72-26
Email: france@oreilly.fr

## CANADA (FRENCH LANGUAGE BOOKS)
Les Éditions Flammarion ltée
375, Avenue Laurier Ouest
Montréal (Québec) H2V 2K3
Tel: 00-1-514-277-8807
Fax: 00-1-514-278-2085
Email: info@flammarion.qc.ca

## HONG KONG
City Discount Subscription Service, Ltd.
Unit A, 6th Floor, Yan's Tower
27 Wong Chuk Hang Road
Aberdeen, Hong Kong
Tel: 852-2580-3539
Fax: 852-2580-6463
Email: citydis@ppn.com.hk

## KOREA
Hanbit Media, Inc.
Chungmu Bldg. 210
Yonnam-dong 568-33
Mapo-gu
Seoul, Korea
Tel: 822-325-0397
Fax: 822-325-9697
Email: hant93@chollian.dacom.co.kr

## PHILIPPINES
Global Publishing
G/F Benavides Garden
1186 Benavides St.
Manila, Philippines
Tel: 632-254-8949/632-252-2582
Fax: 632-734-5060/632-252-2733
Email: globalp@pacific.net.ph

## TAIWAN
O'Reilly Taiwan
1st Floor, No. 21, Lane 295
Section 1, Fu-Shing South Road
Taipei, 106 Taiwan
Tel: 886-2-27099669
Fax: 886-2-27038802
Email: mori@oreilly.com

## CHINA
O'Reilly Beijing
SIGMA Building, Suite B809
No. 49 Zhichun Road
Haidian District
Beijing 100031, P.R. China
Tel: 86-10-8809-7475
Fax: 86-10-8809-7463
Email: beijing@oreilly.com

## INDIA
Shroff Publishers & Distributors Pvt. Ltd.
12, "Roseland", 2nd Floor
180, Waterfield Road, Bandra (West)
Mumbai 400 050
Tel: 91-22-641-1800/643-9910
Fax: 91-22-643-2422
Email: spd@vsnl.com

## JAPAN
O'Reilly Japan, Inc.
Yotsuya Y's Building
7 Banch 6, Honshio-cho
Shinjuku-ku
Tokyo 160-0003 Japan
Tel: 81-3-3356-5227
Fax: 81-3-3356-5261
Email: japan@oreilly.com

## SINGAPORE, INDONESIA, MALAYSIA AND THAILAND
TransQuest Publishers Pte Ltd
30 Old Toh Tuck Road #05-02
Sembawang Kimtrans Logistics Centre
Singapore 597654
Tel: 65-4623112
Fax: 65-4625761
Email: wendiw@transquest.com.sg

## ALL OTHER ASIAN COUNTRIES
O'Reilly & Associates, Inc.
101 Morris Street
Sebastopol, CA 95472 USA
Tel: 707-829-0515
Fax: 707-829-0104
Email: order@oreilly.com

## AUSTRALIA
Woodslane Pty., Ltd.
7/5 Vuko Place
Warriewood NSW 2102
Australia
Tel: 61-2-9970-5111
Fax: 61-2-9970-5002
Email: info@woodslane.com.au

## NEW ZEALAND
Woodslane New Zealand, Ltd.
21 Cooks Street (P.O. Box 575)
Waganui, New Zealand
Tel: 64-6-347-6543
Fax: 64-6-345-4840
Email: info@woodslane.com.au

## ARGENTINA
Distribuidora Cuspide
Suipacha 764
1008 Buenos Aires
Argentina
Phone: 5411-4322-8868
Fax: 5411-4322-3456
Email: libros@cuspide.com

## O'REILLY®